Rec'd March

The DAILY BIBLE®
Devotional
Journal

F. LaGard Smith

HARVEST HOUSE PUBLISHERS

EUGENE, OREGON

Cover by Koechel Peterson & Associates, Inc., Minneapolis, Minnesota

THE DAILY BIBLE® DEVOTIONAL JOURNAL

Published by Harvest House Publishers
Eugene, Oregon 97402
www.harvesthousepublishers.com

ISBN-13: 978-0-7369-1912-8
ISBN-10: 0-7369-1912-0

Printed in the United States of America

06 07 08 09 10 11 12 13 14 / LB-CF / 10 9 8 7 6 5 4 3 2 1

INTRODUCTION TO
THE DAILY BIBLE DEVOTIONAL JOURNAL

Welcome to *The Daily Bible Devotional Journal*, your path and guide to an exhilarating year of spiritual feasting in God's Word. Nothing quite compares with a combination of God's divine inspiration and your own personal reflections.

You can experience a wonderful fourfold blessing by keeping a daily journal. First, the ingrained practice of journaling each day ensures that you won't easily abandon your daily Bible reading. Second, journaling helps you read at the deepest possible level—not just in your mind, but in the reflective depths of your innermost soul. Third, you will have a benchmark to look back on when in future years you wish to trace your spiritual growth along a faith journey of a lifetime. And perhaps most importantly, your journal could well become a perfect talking point for sharing the good news with those who might never read God's Word for themselves.

Spiritual journals of many kinds are available, but none is quite like this one. The reading plan in this journal matches *The Daily Bible*, so it is arranged chronologically from beginning to end. The resulting tapestry is an unfolding story of the history of God's dealing with man from Creation to the patriarchs, from the nation of Israel with its laws, proverbs, and psalms to the ancient prophets and their role in the turbulent history of Israel, and finally from the culmination of God's plan in the person of Jesus of Nazareth to the establishment of His body of believers on earth, as directed in the first century by Christ's Spirit-led apostles. To read chronologically is to improve your understanding both logically and theologically. More yet, it helps you feel the working presence of God in your life even today…and every day.

As you probably know, certain passages of Scriptures are virtually duplicated (as in the Kings and Chronicles), or are presented to us from the viewpoint of different writers (as in the four Gospels). Where similar, parallel accounts exist, we have chosen the day's reading from the fullest account possible, but you may wish to read the complete text for yourself. If so, those additional passages are listed for your convenience at the bottom of the page.

With each day's reading, you will be prompted to answer four simple questions:

+ What key events, teaching, or concepts are revealed in your reading?

+ What verse or verses seem to be the key to the passage at hand?

+ What is God telling you about Himself and your relationship with Him?

+ How can you apply what you have read to the events and activities of your day?

The first question is designed to help you get to the heart and soul of the passage in its proper context. Whether the particular genre is history, law, poetry, or prophecy, surely the inspired writer penned the words to his original audience for a specific reason. Can you tell what that is? Do you understand the words in the same way the original readers would have understood them? To miss the meaning is to miss the message.

The second question should help focus your reading so that you don't get distracted by all the potential rabbit-trails tempting you away from the main point. Finding key verses also allows you to memorize a thought or idea that you can carry with you for a lifetime.

The third question brings you into the very presence of God. It causes you to be still and listen to your Creator and God as He speaks to you personally. No one else—just you. If it were possible to have a one-on-one conversation with God, would you not drop everything else to hear what He has to say? On this side of eternity, this may be your best possible opportunity!

The final question makes your reading and journaling more than just an academic exercise. It will literally change each day of your life as you seek to apply your reading in some specific, practical way. Important relationships will never be the same. Work and school and family life will be vitally transformed as you let God become your daily companion. Walking in your real world. Healing your real hurts. Taking your dreams and hopes and making them soar!

As compiler and narrator of *The Daily Bible*, I hope you will come to share the joy of reading and journaling as never before. May God richly bless your life in the Word...and in each moment of reflection in your heart.

F. LaGard Smith

THE DAILY BIBLE METHOD

1. *Read the Bible each day.* Reading the Bible in chronological order makes the biblical story really come alive. This daily reading schedule also promotes good reading habits and helps get you through some of the more difficult, or perhaps less exciting, parts of the Bible.

2. *Hit more than you miss.* Of course, you will want to read your Bible every day. That's always the goal. But if you've read five days and missed two, you've still won! The idea is to encourage your reading without being unrealistic about your schedule. Your family, church, work, and school activities make lots of demands on you.

3. *Mark it up.* Using a red pen, mark anything of interest that pops up during your reading. If you have a question, big question marks are in order. If something hits your funny bone, draw a happy face in the margin. If a special memory, or a prayer, or a particular concern comes to mind, notes in the margin will help you remember those thoughts so you can expand on them in your journal. The idea is not simply to read the text but to interact with it in an intimate way.

4. *Understand the point.* As you read, try to understand what the text is saying to its original readers. Remember that virtually every biblical passage addresses some kind of spiritual problem and offers an appropriate solution. So the first question to ask with each reading is this: In

their historical context, what did these words mean to their very first readers?

5. *Apply the point.* The Bible is not meant just for people who lived centuries ago, so the second question is this: How do these verses apply to me? Even if the reading for the day is about all the minute building regulations for construction of the tabernacle, or is a seemingly boring genealogy of Jesus' ancestors, or perhaps a detailed description of which tribes got what part of the Promised Land—you can always find something to apply to your daily life. In a way that otherwise might seem selfish, dig into the Word and get what you can for yourself!

6. *Pray the point.* Now pray about what you've read, either at night or the next day. Prayer will keep alive what you've read and move the message from your head to your heart. The message will extend from yourself to others as you begin to "pray the point" on behalf of other people.

7. *Share the point.* Tell others what made you laugh or maybe even cry. Did you consider something you'd never thought about before? Don't be shy. You don't have to be a Bible scholar to share what you've learned. And don't forget to listen to what others are learning.

JANUARY 1

The Daily Bible pages 1–6

Genesis 1–3

Key events, teaching, or concept:

Key verses:

What is God telling me about Himself or my relationship with Him?

How does this apply to my life today?

The Daily Bible pages 6–10

Genesis 4–5

Key events, teaching, or concept:

_____

_____

_____

_____

_____

Key verses:

_____

_____

_____

What is God telling me about Himself or my relationship with Him?

_____

_____

_____

_____

How does this apply to my life today?

_____

_____

_____

JANUARY 3

The Daily Bible **pages 11–16**

Genesis 6–9

Key events, teaching, or concept:

Key verses:

What is God telling me about Himself or my relationship with Him?

How does this apply to my life today?

JANUARY 4

The Daily Bible pages 17–22

Genesis 10–11

Key events, teaching, or concept:

Key verses:

What is God telling me about Himself or my relationship with Him?

How does this apply to my life today?

JANUARY 5

The Daily Bible pages 23–28

Genesis 12–14

Key events, teaching, or concept:

_____

_____

_____

_____

_____

Key verses:

_____

_____

_____

What is God telling me about Himself or my relationship with Him?

_____

_____

_____

_____

How does this apply to my life today?

_____

_____

_____

JANUARY 6

The Daily Bible **pages 29–34**

Genesis 15–17

Key events, teaching, or concept:

_____

_____

_____

_____

_____

Key verses:

_____

_____

_____

What is God telling me about Himself or my relationship with Him?

_____

_____

_____

_____

How does this apply to my life today?

_____

_____

_____

JANUARY 7

The Daily Bible **pages 34–39**

Genesis 18–19

Key events, teaching, or concept:

Key verses:

What is God telling me about Himself or my relationship with Him?

How does this apply to my life today?

JANUARY 8

The Daily Bible **pages 39–44**

Genesis 20–21

Key events, teaching, or concept:

_____

_____

_____

_____

_____

Key verses:

_____

_____

_____

What is God telling me about Himself or my relationship with Him?

_____

_____

_____

_____

How does this apply to my life today?

_____

_____

_____

JANUARY 9

The Daily Bible **pages 44–47**

Genesis 22–23

Key events, teaching, or concept:

Key verses:

What is God telling me about Himself or my relationship with Him?

How does this apply to my life today?

JANUARY 10

The Daily Bible pages 47–50

Genesis 24

Key events, teaching, or concept:

Key verses:

What is God telling me about Himself or my relationship with Him?

How does this apply to my life today?

JANUARY 11

The Daily Bible pages 50–55

Genesis 25:1–26:33

Key events, teaching, or concept:

_____

_____

_____

_____

Key verses:

_____

_____

What is God telling me about Himself or my relationship with Him?

_____

_____

_____

How does this apply to my life today?

_____

_____

_____

JANUARY 12

The Daily Bible **pages 55–59**

Genesis 26:34–28:22

Key events, teaching, or concept:

Key verses:

What is God telling me about Himself or my relationship with Him?

How does this apply to my life today?

JANUARY 13

Key events, teaching, or concept:

Key verses:

What is God telling me about Himself or my relationship with Him?

How does this apply to my life today?

JANUARY 14

The Daily Bible **pages 63–68**

Genesis 31–33

Key events, teaching, or concept:

_____

_____

_____

_____

_____

Key verses:

_____

_____

_____

What is God telling me about Himself or my relationship with Him?

_____

_____

_____

_____

How does this apply to my life today?

_____

_____

_____

JANUARY 15

The Daily Bible **pages 68–71**

Genesis 34–35

Key events, teaching, or concept:

Key verses:

What is God telling me about Himself or my relationship with Him?

How does this apply to my life today?

JANUARY 16

The Daily Bible pages 71–74

Genesis 36

Key events, teaching, or concept:

_____

_____

_____

_____

_____

Key verses:

_____

_____

_____

What is God telling me about Himself or my relationship with Him?

_____

_____

_____

_____

How does this apply to my life today?

_____

_____

_____

_____

JANUARY 17

The Daily Bible pages 74–78

Genesis 37–38

Key events, teaching, or concept:

_____

_____

_____

_____

_____

Key verses:

_____

_____

_____

What is God telling me about Himself or my relationship with Him?

_____

_____

_____

_____

How does this apply to my life today?

_____

_____

_____

JANUARY 18

The Daily Bible **pages 78–82**

Genesis 39:1–42:5

Key events, teaching, or concept:

Key verses:

What is God telling me about Himself or my relationship with Him?

How does this apply to my life today?

JANUARY 19

The Daily Bible pages 82–87

Genesis 42:6–45:15

Key events, teaching, or concept:

_____

_____

_____

_____

_____

Key verses:

_____

_____

_____

What is God telling me about Himself or my relationship with Him?

_____

_____

_____

_____

How does this apply to my life today?

_____

_____

_____

JANUARY 20

The Daily Bible pages 87–91

Genesis 45:16–47:28

Key events, teaching, or concept:

_____

_____

_____

_____

_____

Key verses:

_____

_____

_____

What is God telling me about Himself or my relationship with Him?

_____

_____

_____

_____

How does this apply to my life today?

_____

_____

_____

JANUARY 21

The Daily Bible pages 91–96

Genesis 47:29–50:26

Key events, teaching, or concept:

_____

_____

_____

_____

_____

Key verses:

_____

_____

_____

What is God telling me about Himself or my relationship with Him?

_____

_____

_____

_____

How does this apply to my life today?

_____

_____

_____

_____

JANUARY 22

The Daily Bible **pages 97–102**

Exodus 1–4; 6:14-27

Key events, teaching, or concept:

_____

_____

_____

_____

_____

Key verses:

_____

_____

_____

What is God telling me about Himself or my relationship with Him?

_____

_____

_____

_____

How does this apply to my life today?

_____

_____

_____

_____

JANUARY 23

The Daily Bible pages 103–107

Exodus 5:1–6:13; 7–8

Key events, teaching, or concept:

_____

_____

_____

_____

_____

Key verses:

_____

_____

_____

What is God telling me about Himself or my relationship with Him?

_____

_____

_____

_____

How does this apply to my life today?

_____

_____

_____

Parallel passages: Exodus 6:28-30

JANUARY 24

The Daily Bible pages 107–110

Exodus 9–11

Key events, teaching, or concept:

_____

_____

_____

_____

Key verses:

_____

_____

_____

What is God telling me about Himself or my relationship with Him?

_____

_____

_____

How does this apply to my life today?

_____

_____

_____

JANUARY 25

The Daily Bible **pages 110–113**

Exodus 12:1-49, 51; 13:1-16

Key events, teaching, or concept:

Key verses:

What is God telling me about Himself or my relationship with Him?

How does this apply to my life today?

Parallel passages: Exodus 12:50

JANUARY 26

The Daily Bible **pages 113–117**

Exodus 13:17–15:21

Key events, teaching, or concept:

Key verses:

What is God telling me about Himself or my relationship with Him?

How does this apply to my life today?

JANUARY 27

The Daily Bible pages 117–121

Exodus 15:22–18:27

Key events, teaching, or concept:

_____

_____

_____

_____

_____

Key verses:

_____

_____

_____

What is God telling me about Himself or my relationship with Him?

_____

_____

_____

_____

How does this apply to my life today?

_____

_____

_____

JANUARY 28

The Daily Bible **pages 121–126**

Exodus 19–20; 23:20-33; 24

Key events, teaching, or concept:

Key verses:

What is God telling me about Himself or my relationship with Him?

How does this apply to my life today?

JANUARY 29

The Daily Bible pages 126–131

Exodus 25–28

Key events, teaching, or concept:

Key verses:

What is God telling me about Himself or my relationship with Him?

How does this apply to my life today?

JANUARY 30

The Daily Bible **pages 131–135**
Exodus 29–31

Key events, teaching, or concept:

_____

_____

_____

_____

_____

Key verses:

_____

_____

_____

What is God telling me about Himself or my relationship with Him?

_____

_____

_____

_____

How does this apply to my life today?

_____

_____

_____

_____

JANUARY 31

The Daily Bible pages 135–139

Exodus 32:1–34:16,27-35

Key events, teaching, or concept:

Key verses:

What is God telling me about Himself or my relationship with Him?

How does this apply to my life today?

FEBRUARY 1

The Daily Bible pages 140–145

Exodus 35:4–39:1

Key events, teaching, or concept:

_____

_____

_____

_____

_____

Key verses:

_____

_____

_____

What is God telling me about Himself or my relationship with Him?

_____

_____

_____

_____

How does this apply to my life today?

_____

_____

_____

FEBRUARY 2

The Daily Bible pages 145–147

Exodus 39:2–40:35

Key events, teaching, or concept:

_____
_____
_____
_____

Key verses:

_____
_____

What is God telling me about Himself or my relationship with Him?

_____
_____
_____

How does this apply to my life today?

_____
_____
_____

FEBRUARY 3

The Daily Bible pages 147–151

Leviticus 8–10

Key events, teaching, or concept:

_____

_____

_____

_____

_____

Key verses:

_____

_____

_____

What is God telling me about Himself or my relationship with Him?

_____

_____

_____

_____

How does this apply to my life today?

_____

_____

_____

FEBRUARY 4

The Daily Bible pages 152–157

Numbers 3:1-13; 7–8

Key events, teaching, or concept:

Key verses:

What is God telling me about Himself or my relationship with Him?

How does this apply to my life today?

FEBRUARY 5

The Daily Bible pages 157–162

Numbers 1–2

Key events, teaching, or concept:

_____

_____

_____

_____

_____

Key verses:

_____

_____

_____

What is God telling me about Himself or my relationship with Him?

_____

_____

_____

_____

How does this apply to my life today?

_____

_____

_____

FEBRUARY 6

Key events, teaching, or concept:

Key verses:

What is God telling me about Himself or my relationship with Him?

How does this apply to my life today?

The Daily Bible pages 166–170
Exodus 40:36-38, Numbers 9:15-23; 10–11

Key events, teaching, or concept:

_____

_____

_____

_____

_____

Key verses:

_____

_____

_____

What is God telling me about Himself or my relationship with Him?

_____

_____

_____

_____

How does this apply to my life today?

_____

_____

_____

_____

FEBRUARY 8

The Daily Bible pages 170–174

Numbers 12–14

Key events, teaching, or concept:

_____

_____

_____

_____

Key verses:

_____

_____

_____

What is God telling me about Himself or my relationship with Him?

_____

_____

_____

_____

How does this apply to my life today?

_____

_____

_____

_____

The Daily Bible pages 174–179

Numbers 16–18

Key events, teaching, or concept:

_____

_____

_____

_____

_____

Key verses:

_____

_____

_____

What is God telling me about Himself or my relationship with Him?

_____

_____

_____

_____

How does this apply to my life today?

_____

_____

_____

_____

FEBRUARY 10

The Daily Bible pages 179–184

Numbers 20–21; 33:1-49

Key events, teaching, or concept:

Key verses:

What is God telling me about Himself or my relationship with Him?

How does this apply to my life today?

FEBRUARY 11

The Daily Bible pages 184–190

Numbers 22–24

Key events, teaching, or concept:

_____

_____

_____

_____

_____

Key verses:

_____

_____

_____

What is God telling me about Himself or my relationship with Him?

_____

_____

_____

_____

How does this apply to my life today?

_____

_____

_____

The Daily Bible pages 190–194

Numbers 25; 31

Key events, teaching, or concept:

_____

_____

_____

_____

_____

Key verses:

_____

_____

_____

What is God telling me about Himself or my relationship with Him?

_____

_____

_____

How does this apply to my life today?

_____

_____

_____

FEBRUARY 13

The Daily Bible pages 194–198

Numbers 26

Key events, teaching, or concept:

_____

_____

_____

_____

_____

Key verses:

_____

_____

_____

What is God telling me about Himself or my relationship with Him?

_____

_____

_____

_____

How does this apply to my life today?

_____

_____

_____

FEBRUARY 14

The Daily Bible **pages 198–203**

Numbers 27:15-23; 32; 33:50-56; Deuteronomy 4:41-43

Key events, teaching, or concept:

Key verses:

What is God telling me about Himself or my relationship with Him?

How does this apply to my life today?

FEBRUARY 15

The Daily Bible pages 203–210

Deuteronomy 1:1–4:40

Key events, teaching, or concept:

_____

_____

_____

_____

_____

Key verses:

_____

_____

_____

What is God telling me about Himself or my relationship with Him?

_____

_____

_____

_____

How does this apply to my life today?

_____

_____

_____

The Daily Bible pages 210–214

Deuteronomy 4:44-49; 5:1-5,22-33; 6–8

Key events, teaching, or concept:

Key verses:

What is God telling me about Himself or my relationship with Him?

How does this apply to my life today?

FEBRUARY 17

The Daily Bible pages 214–218

Deuteronomy 9–11

Key events, teaching, or concept:

_____

_____

_____

_____

_____

Key verses:

_____

_____

_____

What is God telling me about Himself or my relationship with Him?

_____

_____

_____

_____

How does this apply to my life today?

_____

_____

_____

_____

FEBRUARY 18

The Daily Bible pages 219–223

Exodus 22:20; 23:13; Leviticus 19:4,27-28; 20:1-5; 26:1;
Deuteronomy 5:5-10; 12:1-15,17-22,26-31; 13:6-18; 14:1-2; 16:21-22

Key events, teaching, or concept:

Key verses:

What is God telling me about Himself or my relationship with Him?

How does this apply to my life today?

Parallel passages: Exodus 34:17; Leviticus 18:21; 26:2

FEBRUARY 19

The Daily Bible pages 223–228

Exodus 22:18,28-30; 23:18-19; 31:12-17; 34:19-21; 35:3;
Leviticus 19:23-25,30; 20:27; 23:1-3; 24:10-16,23; Numbers 15:32-36;
Deuteronomy 5:11-15; 13:1-5; 14:22-29; 15:19-23; 18:1-22; 26:1-15

Key events, teaching, or concept:

Key verses:

What is God telling me about Himself or my relationship with Him?

How does this apply to my life today?

Parallel passages: Exodus 23:12; 34:26; 35:1-2;
Leviticus 19:3,26,31; 20:6-8; 26:2

FEBRUARY 20

The Daily Bible pages 228–236

Exodus 23:14-17; 34:24; Leviticus 16; 23:4-21,26-44; 26:36-44;
Numbers 9:13-14; 28:18-31; 29:1-38; Deuteronomy 16:1-7,9-17

Key events, teaching, or concept:

Key verses:

What is God telling me about Himself or my relationship with Him?

How does this apply to my life today?

Parallel passages: Exodus 34:18,22-23; Leviticus 23:23-25;
Numbers 28:16-17; 29:39-40; Deuteronomy 16:8

The Daily Bible **pages 236–240**

Leviticus 1–2; 6:8-23; 17:8-9; Numbers 15:1-21; 28:1-8

Key events, teaching, or concept:

Key verses:

What is God telling me about Himself or my relationship with Him?

How does this apply to my life today?

FEBRUARY 22

The Daily Bible **pages 240–245**

Leviticus 3–4; 5:1-13; 6:24-30; 7:11-21,28-36; 17:1-7; Numbers 15:29-31

Key events, teaching, or concept:

Key verses:

What is God telling me about Himself or my relationship with Him?

How does this apply to my life today?

Parallel passages: Numbers 15:27-28

FEBRUARY 23

The Daily Bible pages 245–248

Exodus 23:18; Leviticus 5:14-19; 6:1-7; 7:1-10,37-38; 22:17-30;
24:1-9; Numbers 6:22-27; 28:9-15; Deuteronomy 21:1-9

Key events, teaching, or concept:

Key verses:

What is God telling me about Himself or my relationship with Him?

How does this apply to my life today?

Parallel passages: Exodus 23:10-11

The Daily Bible pages 248–252

Exodus 23:10-11; Leviticus 21:1–22:16; 25:1-34,39-43,47-55

Key events, teaching, or concept:

Key verses:

What is God telling me about Himself or my relationship with Him?

How does this apply to my life today?

FEBRUARY 25

The Daily Bible pages 252–256

Leviticus 12:1-8; 14:1-32; 15:13-15,28-30; Numbers 19:1-22

Key events, teaching, or concept:

Key verses:

What is God telling me about Himself or my relationship with Him?

How does this apply to my life today?

FEBRUARY 26

The Daily Bible pages 256–261

Leviticus 19:1-2,19; 27:1-34; Numbers 6:1-21; Deuteronomy 22:9-11; 23:1-8,21-23

Key events, teaching, or concept:

Key verses:

What is God telling me about Himself or my relationship with Him?

How does this apply to my life today?

Parallel passages: Numbers 30:1-16; Leviticus 22:9

FEBRUARY 27

The Daily Bible pages 261–263

Exodus 22:28; 23:1-2,7-8; Leviticus 19:15;
Deuteronomy 5:20; 16:18-20; 17:8-20; 19:15-21; 21:22-23; 24:16; 25:1-3

Key events, teaching, or concept:

Key verses:

What is God telling me about Himself or my relationship with Him?

How does this apply to my life today?

Parallel passages: Exodus 23:3,6; Deuteronomy 1:9-18

FEBRUARY 28

The Daily Bible pages 263–267

Exodus 21:12-27; 22:1-4; Leviticus 24:19-20; Numbers 33:34; 35:9-34;
Deuteronomy 5:17,19; 19:1-14; 22:25-29; 24:7; 25:11-12

Key events, teaching, or concept:

Key verses:

What is God telling me about Himself or my relationship with Him?

How does this apply to my life today?

Parallel passages: Leviticus 24:17,21

MARCH 1

The Daily Bible pages 267–274

Exodus 21:28-36; 22:5-17; Leviticus 19:11-12,35-37; 24:18; 25:44-46;
Numbers 5:5-10; 27:1-11; 30:1-16; 36:1-13; Deuteronomy 15:1-18;
21:15-17; 23:15-16,19-20; 24:14-15; 25:5-10,13-16

Key events, teaching, or concept:

Key verses:

What is God telling me about Himself or my relationship with Him?

How does this apply to my life today?

Parallel passages: Leviticus 19:13; 24:21

MARCH 2

The Daily Bible pages 274–280

Leviticus 18:1-20,22-30; 19:20-22,29; 20:11-22,24; Numbers 5:11-31;
Deuteronomy 5:18; 21:10-14; 22:5,13-24; 23:17-18; 24:1-5

Key events, teaching, or concept:

Key verses:

What is God telling me about Himself or my relationship with Him?

How does this apply to my life today?

The Daily Bible pages 280–285

Leviticus 13; 14:33-57; 15:1-12,16-27,31-33; Numbers 5:1-4; Deuteronomy 24:8-9

Key events, teaching, or concept:

_____

_____

_____

_____

_____

Key verses:

_____

_____

_____

What is God telling me about Himself or my relationship with Him?

_____

_____

_____

_____

How does this apply to my life today?

_____

_____

_____

_____

Parallel passages: Exodus 22:19; Leviticus 20:10, 22-23; Deuteronomy 22:30

MARCH 4

The Daily Bible pages 285–288

Exodus 22:31; 23:19; Leviticus 7:22-25; 11:4-47;
17:10-16; 20:25-26; Deuteronomy 14:3-5,21

Key events, teaching, or concept:

Key verses:

What is God telling me about Himself or my relationship with Him?

How does this apply to my life today?

Parallel passages: Exodus 34:26; Leviticus 7:26-27; 11:1-3;
19:26; Deuteronomy 12:16,23-25; 14:6-21

MARCH 5

The Daily Bible pages 288–292

Exodus 22:22-24; Leviticus 19:3,9-10,14-18,32-34; 20:9; 24:22; 25:35-38;
Deuteronomy 5:16,21; 20:1-20; 21:18-21; 22:1-4,6-7; 23:9-14,24-25; 24:19-22; 25:4

Key events, teaching, or concept:

_____

_____

_____

_____

Key verses:

_____

_____

What is God telling me about Himself or my relationship with Him?

_____

_____

_____

How does this apply to my life today?

_____

_____

_____

Parallel passages: Exodus 21:17; 22:21; 23:4-5,9;
Leviticus 23:22; Deuteronomy 21:10-14; 24:5

MARCH 6

The Daily Bible pages 292–295

Leviticus 22:31-33; 26:3-46; Numbers 15:37-41; Deuteronomy 12:32; 31:9-13

Key events, teaching, or concept:

Key verses:

What is God telling me about Himself or my relationship with Him?

How does this apply to my life today?

Parallel passages: Deuteronomy 22:12

MARCH 7

The Daily Bible pages 296–302

Deuteronomy 26:16–30:20

Key events, teaching, or concept:

_____

_____

_____

_____

_____

Key verses:

_____

_____

_____

What is God telling me about Himself or my relationship with Him?

_____

_____

_____

_____

How does this apply to my life today?

_____

_____

_____

_____

MARCH 8

The Daily Bible **pages 303–308**

Deuteronomy 31:1-8,14–32:47

Key events, teaching, or concept:

_____

_____

_____

_____

_____

Key verses:

_____

_____

_____

What is God telling me about Himself or my relationship with Him?

_____

_____

_____

_____

How does this apply to my life today?

_____

_____

_____

MARCH 9

The Daily Bible pages 308–312

Deuteronomy 32:48–34:12

Key events, teaching, or concept:

_____

_____

_____

_____

_____

Key verses:

_____

_____

_____

What is God telling me about Himself or my relationship with Him?

_____

_____

_____

_____

How does this apply to my life today?

_____

_____

_____

_____

Parallel passages: Numbers 27:12-14

MARCH 10

The Daily Bible pages 312–317

Joshua 1–5

Key events, teaching, or concept:

Key verses:

What is God telling me about Himself or my relationship with Him?

How does this apply to my life today?

MARCH 11

The Daily Bible pages 317–322

Joshua 6–8

Key events, teaching, or concept:

_____

_____

_____

_____

_____

Key verses:

_____

_____

_____

What is God telling me about Himself or my relationship with Him?

_____

_____

_____

_____

How does this apply to my life today?

_____

_____

_____

MARCH 12

The Daily Bible pages 322–328

Joshua 9–12

Key events, teaching, or concept:

Key verses:

What is God telling me about Himself or my relationship with Him?

How does this apply to my life today?

Parallel passages: Joshua 14:15

MARCH 13

The Daily Bible pages 328–333

Joshua 13:1-12,14-33; 14:1–15:12,20-62; 16:1-9; 17:1-10,14-18

Key events, teaching, or concept:

Key verses:

What is God telling me about Himself or my relationship with Him?

How does this apply to my life today?

Parallel passages: Judges 1:20

MARCH 14

The Daily Bible pages 333–338

Joshua 18–21

Key events, teaching, or concept:

Key verses:

What is God telling me about Himself or my relationship with Him?

How does this apply to my life today?

MARCH 15

The Daily Bible **pages 338–343**

Joshua 22:1–24:28

Key events, teaching, or concept:

_____

_____

_____

_____

Key verses:

_____

_____

What is God telling me about Himself or my relationship with Him?

_____

_____

_____

How does this apply to my life today?

_____

_____

_____

Parallel passages: Judges 2:6

MARCH 16

The Daily Bible **pages 343–346**

Joshua 13:13; 15:13-14,63; 16:10; 17:11-13; 24:32-33; Judges 1:1-26,30-36; 2:1-5,8-9

Key events, teaching, or concept:

Key verses:

What is God telling me about Himself or my relationship with Him?

How does this apply to my life today?

Parallel passages: Joshua 15:15-19; 24:29-30; Judges 1:20,27-29

MARCH 17

The Daily Bible **pages 346–349**

Judges 2:7,10-23–3:31

Key events, teaching, or concept:

Key verses:

What is God telling me about Himself or my relationship with Him?

How does this apply to my life today?

Parallel passages: Joshua 24:31

MARCH 18

The Daily Bible pages 349–353

Judges 4–5

Key events, teaching, or concept:

Key verses:

What is God telling me about Himself or my relationship with Him?

How does this apply to my life today?

The Daily Bible pages 353–357

Judges 6:1–8:3

Key events, teaching, or concept:

_____

_____

_____

_____

_____

Key verses:

_____

_____

_____

What is God telling me about Himself or my relationship with Him?

_____

_____

_____

_____

How does this apply to my life today?

_____

_____

_____

MARCH 20

The Daily Bible pages 357–361

Judges 8:4-35; 9:1-57

Key events, teaching, or concept:

Key verses:

What is God telling me about Himself or my relationship with Him?

How does this apply to my life today?

MARCH 21

The Daily Bible pages 361–364

Judges 10–12

Key events, teaching, or concept:

_____
_____
_____
_____
_____

Key verses:

_____
_____
_____

What is God telling me about Himself or my relationship with Him?

_____
_____
_____
_____

How does this apply to my life today?

_____
_____
_____

MARCH 22

The Daily Bible pages 365–369

Ruth

Key events, teaching, or concept:

_____

_____

_____

_____

_____

Key verses:

_____

_____

_____

What is God telling me about Himself or my relationship with Him?

_____

_____

_____

_____

How does this apply to my life today?

_____

_____

_____

MARCH 23

The Daily Bible pages 369–375

Judges 12–16

Key events, teaching, or concept:

_____

_____

_____

_____

_____

Key verses:

_____

_____

_____

What is God telling me about Himself or my relationship with Him?

_____

_____

_____

_____

How does this apply to my life today?

_____

_____

_____

_____

MARCH 24

The Daily Bible pages 375–378

Judges 17–18

Key events, teaching, or concept:

_____

_____

_____

_____

_____

Key verses:

_____

_____

_____

What is God telling me about Himself or my relationship with Him?

_____

_____

_____

_____

How does this apply to my life today?

_____

_____

_____

_____

MARCH 25

The Daily Bible pages 378–383

Judges 19–21

Key events, teaching, or concept:

Key verses:

What is God telling me about Himself or my relationship with Him?

How does this apply to my life today?

MARCH 26

The Daily Bible pages 384–387

1 Samuel 1–2

Key events, teaching, or concept:

Key verses:

What is God telling me about Himself or my relationship with Him?

How does this apply to my life today?

The Daily Bible pages 388–392

1 Samuel 3–7

Key events, teaching, or concept:

Key verses:

What is God telling me about Himself or my relationship with Him?

How does this apply to my life today?

The Daily Bible pages 392–398

1 Samuel 8–12

Key events, teaching, or concept:

Key verses:

What is God telling me about Himself or my relationship with Him?

How does this apply to my life today?

MARCH 29

The Daily Bible pages 398–402

1 Samuel 13–14:45,49-51; 1 Chronicles 9:35-44

Key events, teaching, or concept:

Key verses:

What is God telling me about Himself or my relationship with Him?

How does this apply to my life today?

MARCH 30

The Daily Bible pages 402–405

1 Samuel 14:46-48,52–15:35; 1 Chronicles 5:10,18-22

Key events, teaching, or concept:

Key verses:

What is God telling me about Himself or my relationship with Him?

How does this apply to my life today?

The Daily Bible pages 405–409
1 Samuel 16–17

Key events, teaching, or concept:

Key verses:

What is God telling me about Himself or my relationship with Him?

How does this apply to my life today?

APRIL 1

The Daily Bible pages 409–415

1 Samuel 18–21; Psalm 59

Key events, teaching, or concept:

Key verses:

What is God telling me about Himself or my relationship with Him?

How does this apply to my life today?

The Daily Bible pages 415–419

1 Samuel 21:7-15; 22:1-5; 1 Chronicles 12:8-18; Psalm 34; 56; 142

Key events, teaching, or concept:

Key verses:

What is God telling me about Himself or my relationship with Him?

How does this apply to my life today?

APRIL 3

The Daily Bible **pages 419–424**

1 Samuel 22:6–24:22; 25:1; Psalm 52; 54; 57; 63

Key events, teaching, or concept:

Key verses:

What is God telling me about Himself or my relationship with Him?

How does this apply to my life today?

The Daily Bible pages 424–431
1 Samuel 25:1–28:2; 29–30; 1 Chronicles 12:1-7,19-22

Key events, teaching, or concept:

_____

_____

_____

_____

_____

Key verses:

_____

_____

_____

What is God telling me about Himself or my relationship with Him?

_____

_____

_____

_____

How does this apply to my life today?

_____

_____

_____

_____

APRIL 5

The Daily Bible pages 431–434

1 Samuel 28:3-25; 31; 2 Samuel 1:1-27; 4:4; 1 Chronicles 10:13-14

Key events, teaching, or concept:

_____

_____

_____

_____

_____

Key verses:

_____

_____

_____

What is God telling me about Himself or my relationship with Him?

_____

_____

_____

_____

How does this apply to my life today?

_____

_____

_____

Parallel passages: 1 Chronicles 10:1-12

APRIL 6

The Daily Bible pages 434–439

2 Samuel 2:1-10,12-31; 3:2-29; 4:1-3,5-12; 5:4-5; 1 Chronicles 12:23-40

Key events, teaching, or concept:

Key verses:

What is God telling me about Himself or my relationship with Him?

How does this apply to my life today?

Parallel passages: 2 Samuel 2:11; 5:1-3; 1 Kings 2:11; 1 Chronicles 3:1-4; 29:26-27

The Daily Bible pages 439–443

2 Samuel 5:6-8,11-12; 6:1-5; 22; 1 Chronicles 11:6-9; 13:1-14; 14:8-17; Psalm 18

Key events, teaching, or concept:

Key verses:

What is God telling me about Himself or my relationship with Him?

How does this apply to my life today?

Parallel passages: 2 Samuel 5:9-10,17-25; 6:1-11; 1 Chronicles 11:4-5; 14:1-2

APRIL 8

The Daily Bible pages 443–448

2 Samuel 6:12; 1 Chronicles 15:1–16:36; Psalm 96; 105

Key events, teaching, or concept:

_____

_____

_____

_____

_____

Key verses:

_____

_____

_____

What is God telling me about Himself or my relationship with Him?

_____

_____

_____

_____

How does this apply to my life today?

_____

_____

_____

_____

Parallel passages: 2 Samuel 6:12-17

APRIL 9

The Daily Bible **pages 448–451**

2 Samuel 6:20-23; 7:4-29; 8:15-18; 9; 1 Chronicles 16:37-43; 17:1-2

Key events, teaching, or concept:

Key verses:

What is God telling me about Himself or my relationship with Him?

How does this apply to my life today?

Parallel passages: 2 Samuel 7:13; 1 Chronicles 17:3-27; 18:14-17

APRIL 10

The Daily Bible pages 451–456

2 Samuel 11:2-27; 12:1-17; 21:15-22; 1 Chronicles 18:1; 19:1-19; Psalm 51; 60

Key events, teaching, or concept:

Key verses:

What is God telling me about Himself or my relationship with Him?

How does this apply to my life today?

Parallel passages: 2 Samuel 8:1; 10:1-19; 1 Chronicles 20:1,4-8

The Daily Bible pages 456–460

1 Samuel 12:26-31; 2 Samuel 8:2-12; 12:18-23; 23:9-17;
1 Chronicles 11:10-14,20-47; 18:12-13

Key events, teaching, or concept:

Key verses:

What is God telling me about Himself or my relationship with Him?

How does this apply to my life today?

Parallel passages: 2 Samuel 8:13-14; 23:8,18-39; 1 Chronicles 11:15-19; 18:2-11; 20:1-3

The Daily Bible pages 460–463

2 Samuel 12:24-25; 13:1–14:24; 1 Chronicles 3:4-9

Key events, teaching, or concept:

_____

_____

_____

_____

_____

Key verses:

_____

_____

_____

What is God telling me about Himself or my relationship with Him?

_____

_____

_____

_____

How does this apply to my life today?

_____

_____

_____

_____

Parallel passages: 2 Samuel 5:13-16; 1 Chronicles 14:37

APRIL 13

The Daily Bible **pages 464–467**

2 Samuel 14:25-33; 15:1–16:14: Psalm 3

Key events, teaching, or concept:

Key verses:

What is God telling me about Himself or my relationship with Him?

How does this apply to my life today?

APRIL 14

The Daily Bible pages 467–471

2 Samuel 16:15–19:4

Key events, teaching, or concept:

_____
_____
_____
_____
_____

Key verses:

_____
_____
_____

What is God telling me about Himself or my relationship with Him?

_____
_____
_____
_____

How does this apply to my life today?

_____
_____
_____

APRIL 15

The Daily Bible pages 471–475

2 Samuel 19:5–20:36

Key events, teaching, or concept:

Key verses:

What is God telling me about Himself or my relationship with Him?

How does this apply to my life today?

APRIL 16

The Daily Bible pages 475–480

2 Samuel 21:1-14; 24:1-9; 1 Chronicles 21–22; Psalm 30

Key events, teaching, or concept:

_____

_____

_____

_____

_____

Key verses:

_____

_____

_____

What is God telling me about Himself or my relationship with Him?

_____

_____

_____

_____

How does this apply to my life today?

_____

_____

_____

Parallel passages: 2 Samuel 24:10-25

The Daily Bible pages 480–485

1 Chronicles 23:1-31; 24:1-19; 25; 26:1-11

Key events, teaching, or concept:

Key verses:

What is God telling me about Himself or my relationship with Him?

How does this apply to my life today?

Parallel passages: 1 Chronicles 24:20-30

APRIL 18

The Daily Bible pages 485–490

1 Chronicles 23:1; 26:12-32; 27:1–29:22

Key events, teaching, or concept:

Key verses:

What is God telling me about Himself or my relationship with Him?

How does this apply to my life today?

APRIL 19

The Daily Bible pages 490–495

Psalm 5; 6; 7; 10; 11

Key events, teaching, or concept:

Key verses:

What is God telling me about Himself or my relationship with Him?

How does this apply to my life today?

APRIL 20

The Daily Bible pages 495–500

Psalm 13; 17; 23; 26; 28; 31

Key events, teaching, or concept:

_____

_____

_____

_____

_____

Key verses:

_____

_____

_____

What is God telling me about Himself or my relationship with Him?

_____

_____

_____

How does this apply to my life today?

_____

_____

_____

The Daily Bible pages 500–504

Psalm 35; 41; 43; 46; 55

Key events, teaching, or concept:

Key verses:

What is God telling me about Himself or my relationship with Him?

How does this apply to my life today?

APRIL 22

The Daily Bible pages 505–508

Psalm 61–62; 64; 69

Key events, teaching, or concept:

_____

_____

_____

_____

_____

Key verses:

_____

_____

_____

What is God telling me about Himself or my relationship with Him?

_____

_____

_____

How does this apply to my life today?

_____

_____

_____

APRIL 23

The Daily Bible pages 508–513

Psalm 70–71; 77; 83; 86

Key events, teaching, or concept:

_____

_____

_____

_____

_____

Key verses:

_____

_____

_____

What is God telling me about Himself or my relationship with Him?

_____

_____

_____

_____

How does this apply to my life today?

_____

_____

_____

_____

APRIL 24

The Daily Bible pages 513–517

Psalm 88; 91; 95; 108–109

Key events, teaching, or concept:

_____

_____

_____

_____

Key verses:

_____

_____

What is God telling me about Himself or my relationship with Him?

_____

_____

_____

How does this apply to my life today?

_____

_____

_____

APRIL 25

The Daily Bible pages 517–520

Psalm 120–121; 140; 143–144

Key events, teaching, or concept:

Key verses:

What is God telling me about Himself or my relationship with Him?

How does this apply to my life today?

APRIL 26

The Daily Bible pages 521–526

Psalm 1; 14–15; 36–37; 39

Key events, teaching, or concept:

Key verses:

What is God telling me about Himself or my relationship with Him?

How does this apply to my life today?

APRIL 27

The Daily Bible pages 526–531

Psalm 40; 49–50; 73

Key events, teaching, or concept:

_____

_____

_____

_____

_____

Key verses:

_____

_____

_____

What is God telling me about Himself or my relationship with Him?

_____

_____

_____

_____

How does this apply to my life today?

_____

_____

_____

APRIL 28

The Daily Bible pages 531–536

Psalm 76; 82; 84; 90; 92; 112; 115

Key events, teaching, or concept:

_____

_____

_____

_____

Key verses:

_____

_____

_____

What is God telling me about Himself or my relationship with Him?

_____

_____

_____

_____

How does this apply to my life today?

_____

_____

_____

APRIL 29

The Daily Bible pages 536–540

Psalm 8–9; 16; 19; 21; 24

Key events, teaching, or concept:

Key verses:

What is God telling me about Himself or my relationship with Him?

How does this apply to my life today?

APRIL 30

The Daily Bible pages 540–546

Psalm 29; 33; 65–68

Key events, teaching, or concept:

Key verses:

What is God telling me about Himself or my relationship with Him?

How does this apply to my life today?

The Daily Bible pages 546–550

Psalm 75; 93–94; 97–100

Key events, teaching, or concept:

_____

_____

_____

_____

_____

Key verses:

_____

_____

_____

What is God telling me about Himself or my relationship with Him?

_____

_____

_____

_____

How does this apply to my life today?

_____

_____

_____

MAY 2

The Daily Bible pages 550–554

Psalm 103–104; 113–114; 117

Key events, teaching, or concept:

Key verses:

What is God telling me about Himself or my relationship with Him?

How does this apply to my life today?

MAY 3

The Daily Bible pages 554–562

Psalm 119

Key events, teaching, or concept:

Key verses:

What is God telling me about Himself or my relationship with Him?

How does this apply to my life today?

MAY 4

The Daily Bible pages 562–566

Psalm 122; 124; 133–136; 138

Key events, teaching, or concept:

_____

_____

_____

_____

_____

Key verses:

_____

_____

_____

What is God telling me about Himself or my relationship with Him?

_____

_____

_____

_____

How does this apply to my life today?

_____

_____

_____

_____

MAY 5

The Daily Bible **pages 566–569**

Psalm 139; 145; 148; 150

Key events, teaching, or concept:

_____

_____

_____

_____

_____

Key verses:

_____

_____

_____

What is God telling me about Himself or my relationship with Him?

_____

_____

_____

_____

How does this apply to my life today?

_____

_____

_____

_____

The Daily Bible pages 570–574

Psalm 4; 12; 20; 25; 32; 38

Key events, teaching, or concept:

_____

_____

_____

_____

_____

Key verses:

_____

_____

_____

What is God telling me about Himself or my relationship with Him?

_____

_____

_____

_____

How does this apply to my life today?

_____

_____

_____

_____

MAY 7

The Daily Bible pages 574–578

Psalm 42; 53; 58; 81; 101

Key events, teaching, or concept:

Key verses:

What is God telling me about Himself or my relationship with Him?

How does this apply to my life today?

The Daily Bible pages 578–580

Psalm 111; 130–131; 141; 146

Key events, teaching, or concept:

_____

_____

_____

_____

_____

Key verses:

_____

_____

_____

What is God telling me about Himself or my relationship with Him?

_____

_____

_____

_____

How does this apply to my life today?

_____

_____

_____

_____

MAY 9

The Daily Bible pages 580–584

Psalm 2; 22; 27

Key events, teaching, or concept:

_____

_____

_____

_____

_____

Key verses:

_____

_____

_____

What is God telling me about Himself or my relationship with Him?

_____

_____

_____

_____

How does this apply to my life today?

_____

_____

_____

The Daily Bible pages 584–587

Psalm 45; 47–48; 72:20; 87; 110

Key events, teaching, or concept:

_____

_____

_____

_____

_____

Key verses:

_____

_____

_____

What is God telling me about Himself or my relationship with Him?

_____

_____

_____

How does this apply to my life today?

_____

_____

_____

MAY 11

The Daily Bible **pages 587–591**

2 Samuel 23:1-7; 1 Kings 1:1-53; 2:1-10; 1 Chronicles 29:23-25,28-30

Key events, teaching, or concept:

Key verses:

What is God telling me about Himself or my relationship with Him?

How does this apply to my life today?

Parallel passages: 1 Kings 2:12; 2 Chronicles 1:1

MAY 12

The Daily Bible pages 591–595

1 Kings 2:13-46; 3:1-3,5-28; 9:16; 2 Chronicles 1:2-6

Key events, teaching, or concept:

Key verses:

What is God telling me about Himself or my relationship with Him?

How does this apply to my life today?

Parallel passages: 1 Kings 3:4; 2 Chronicles 1:7-13

MAY 13

The Daily Bible **pages 596–602**

1 Kings 5:1-18; 6:1-2,4-13,15-38; 7:13-22,27-51;
2 Chronicles 2:1–3:2,4-14; 4:1-10,19-22; 8:12-16

Key events, teaching, or concept:

Key verses:

What is God telling me about Himself or my relationship with Him?

How does this apply to my life today?

Parallel passages: 1 Kings 6:3,9,14,23-28; 7:23-26,39;
9:25; 2 Chronicles 3:3,7,15-17; 4:11-18; 5:1

The Daily Bible pages 602–606

1 Kings 8:46-61; 2 Chronicles 5:2-14; 6:1-35,40-42; 7:1-10

Key events, teaching, or concept:

Key verses:

What is God telling me about Himself or my relationship with Him?

How does this apply to my life today?

Parallel passages: 1 Kings 8:1-45,62-66; 2 Chronicles 6:36-39

MAY 15

The Daily Bible pages 606–613

1 Kings 4:1-34; 7:1-12; 9:10-15,20-23,26-28; 10:1-25,27;
2 Chronicles 7:11-22; 8:1-6,11; Psalm 72:1-19

Key events, teaching, or concept:

_____

_____

_____

_____

Key verses:

_____

_____

What is God telling me about Himself or my relationship with Him?

_____

_____

_____

How does this apply to my life today?

_____

_____

_____

Parallel passages: 1 Kings 9:1-9,17-19,24; 2 Chronicles 1:14-17; 8:7-10,17-18; 9:1-3

The Daily Bible pages 613–619

Proverbs 1:20-33; 2; 3:13-24; 4; 8:1–9:6,13-18

Key events, teaching, or concept:

Key verses:

What is God telling me about Himself or my relationship with Him?

How does this apply to my life today?

MAY 17

The Daily Bible pages 619–624

Proverbs 1:1-7; 3:5-8; 9:10-12; 10:13-14,23,27; 13:14-16; 14:2,6,8,12,15,18,24,26-27,33;
15:3,14,21,24,33; 16:1,3-4,9,16,20,22,33; 17:12,14; 18:2,4,10,15; 19:2-3,8,21,23;
21:11,22,30-31; 22:12,17-21; 23:12; 24:3-4,7,13-14; 25:1; 26:4-12; 27:1,22; 28:14,26; 29:9,25

Key events, teaching, or concept:

Key verses:

What is God telling me about Himself or my relationship with Him?

How does this apply to my life today?

Parallel passages: Proverbs 16:25

The Daily Bible pages 624–630

Proverbs 3:1-2,11-12,33-35; 9:7-9; 10:3,6-9,16-17,22,24-25,28-30; 11:5-10,14,
18-21,23,27,30-31; 12:1-3,5-8,12,15,21,28; 13:1,6,9,13,18,21,24,25;
14:9,11,14,19,22,34; 15:5-6,9-10,12,22,26,31-32; 16:7; 17:10,13; 18:3;
19:16,18,20,25,27,29; 20:7,18,30; 21:8,12,16,18,21; 22:6,8,15; 23:9,13-14; 24:5-6,
8-9,15-16; 25:12; 26:1,3,27; 27:5-6,17; 28:4,7,9,12-13,18,28; 29:1-2,10,15-17,19,21,27

Key events, teaching, or concept:

_____

_____

_____

_____

_____

Key verses:

_____

_____

_____

What is God telling me about Himself or my relationship with Him?

_____

_____

_____

How does this apply to my life today?

_____

_____

_____

The Daily Bible pages 630–634

Proverbs 3:3-4; 6:12-15; 10:10-12; 11:2-3,16-17; 12:9-10,25;
13:7,10; 14:30; 15:8,11,17,25,29; 16:2,5-6,18-19,30; 17:3,5; 18:1,12;
19:10; 20:6,9,11,14,27; 21:2-4,10,24,27; 22:4; 23:6-8; 24:17-20;
25:16-17,19,21-22,27; 26:16,23-26; 27:2,4,19,21; 28:25; 29:23

Key events, teaching, or concept:

_____

_____

_____

_____

_____

Key verses:

_____

_____

_____

What is God telling me about Himself or my relationship with Him?

_____

_____

_____

_____

How does this apply to my life today?

_____

_____

_____

_____

The Daily Bible pages 634–639

Proverbs 5:1-14,21-23; 6:20–7:27; 12:16; 14:16-17,29; 15:18; 16:32; 19:11,19;
20:1,25; 22:14,24-25; 23:19-21,26-35; 25:8,28; 29:2-3,8,11,20,22

Key events, teaching, or concept:

Key verses:

What is God telling me about Himself or my relationship with Him?

How does this apply to my life today?

MAY 21

The Daily Bible pages 639–642

Proverbs 10:18-21,31-32; 11:11-13; 12:13-14,18-19,22-23; 13:2-3; 14:3;
15:1-2,4,7,23,28; 16:21,23-24,27-28; 17:4,9,14,19-20,27-28; 18:6-8,13,20-21; 19:1,5,22;
20:3,19; 21:6,23; 22:10; 23:15-16; 25:11,14,23; 26:2,20-21,28; 27:14; 28:23; 29:5

Key events, teaching, or concept:

Key verses:

What is God telling me about Himself or my relationship with Him?

How does this apply to my life today?

Parallel passages: Proverbs 26:22

MAY 22

The Daily Bible pages 643–646

Proverbs 1:10-19; 3:29-32; 6:16-19; 10:2; 11:1; 12:17,20; 13:5,11; 14:5,25; 15:27; 16:11,29; 17:1,8,15,23,26; 18:5,17-10; 19:9,28; 20:10,17,21-23; 21:7,14-15,28-29; 22:28; 23:10-11; 24:11-12,23-26,28-29; 25:18,26; 26:17-19; 27:3; 28:5,10,17; 29:26

Key events, teaching, or concept:

_____

_____

_____

_____

Key verses:

_____

_____

_____

What is God telling me about Himself or my relationship with Him?

_____

_____

_____

How does this apply to my life today?

_____

_____

_____

The Daily Bible pages 647–652

Proverbs 3:9-10,27-28; 6:1-11; 10:4-5,15,26; 11:4,15,24-26,28; 12:11,24,27;
13:4,8,22-23; 14:4,20-21,23,31; 15:15-16,19; 16:8,26; 17:16,18; 18:9,11,16,23;
19:4,6-7,15,17,24; 20:4,13,16; 21:13,17,20,25-26; 22:2,7,9,16-17,22-23,26,29;
23:4-5; 24:27,20-24; 25:14; 26:14; 27:8,18,23-27; 28:6,8,11,19-22; 29:7,13

Key events, teaching, or concept:

Key verses:

What is God telling me about Himself or my relationship with Him?

How does this apply to my life today?

Parallel passages: Proverbs 26:15; 27:13

The Daily Bible pages 652–657

Proverbs 1:8-9; 3:25-26; 10:1; 11:22,29; 12:4,26; 13:12,17,19-20; 14:1,7,28,32,35;
15:20; 16:10,12-15,17,31; 17:2,6-7,11,17,21,25; 18:22,24; 19:12-14,26;
20:2,8,20,26,28-29; 21:1,9,19; 22:1,3,5,11,13; 23:1-3,17-18,22-25; 24:1-2,10,21-22;
25:2-7,9-10,13; 26:13; 27:8-10,15-16; 28:1-3,15-16,24; 29:9,12,14,24

Key events, teaching, or concept:

Key verses:

What is God telling me about Himself or my relationship with Him?

How does this apply to my life today?

Parallel passages: Proverbs 25:24; 27:12

MAY 25

The Daily Bible pages 657–661

Proverbs 14:10,13; 15:13,30; 17:22; 18:14; 25:20,25; 27:11,20; 29:6; 30–31

Key events, teaching, or concept:

_____

_____

_____

_____

_____

Key verses:

_____

_____

_____

What is God telling me about Himself or my relationship with Him?

_____

_____

_____

_____

How does this apply to my life today?

_____

_____

_____

MAY 26

The Daily Bible pages 661–672

Psalm 127; Song of Songs

Key events, teaching, or concept:

_____

_____

_____

_____

_____

Key verses:

_____

_____

_____

What is God telling me about Himself or my relationship with Him?

_____

_____

_____

_____

How does this apply to my life today?

_____

_____

_____

_____

MAY 27

The Daily Bible pages 672–674

1 Kings 11:1-40

Key events, teaching, or concept:

Key verses:

What is God telling me about Himself or my relationship with Him?

How does this apply to my life today?

MAY 28

The Daily Bible pages 674–678

Ecclesiastes 1:1-11; 2:12-16; 3:18-22; 6:10-12; 8:16-17; 9:1-12

Key events, teaching, or concept:

_____

_____

_____

_____

_____

Key verses:

_____

_____

_____

What is God telling me about Himself or my relationship with Him?

_____

_____

_____

_____

How does this apply to my life today?

_____

_____

_____

_____

The Daily Bible pages 678–684

Ecclesiastes 1:12-18; 2:1-11,17-26; 4:1–6:9; 7:13-14; 8:2-15; 9:13-18

Key events, teaching, or concept:

_____

_____

_____

_____

_____

Key verses:

_____

_____

_____

_____

What is God telling me about Himself or my relationship with Him?

_____

_____

_____

_____

How does this apply to my life today?

_____

_____

_____

_____

The Daily Bible pages 684–687

Ecclesiastes 7:1-12,15-29; 8:1; 10:1–11:6; 12:9-12

Key events, teaching, or concept:

_____

_____

_____

_____

_____

Key verses:

_____

_____

_____

What is God telling me about Himself or my relationship with Him?

_____

_____

_____

_____

How does this apply to my life today?

_____

_____

_____

MAY 31

The Daily Bible **pages 687–689**

2 Chronicles 9:29-31; Ecclesiastes 3:1-17; 11:7–12:8,13-14

Key events, teaching, or concept:

Key verses:

What is God telling me about Himself or my relationship with Him?

How does this apply to my life today?

Parallel passages: 1 Kings 11:41-43

JUNE 1

The Daily Bible pages 690–694

1 Kings 12:1–13:32; 2 Chronicles 11:13-14,16-17

Key events, teaching, or concept:

Key verses:

What is God telling me about Himself or my relationship with Him?

How does this apply to my life today?

Parallel passages: 2 Chronicles 10:1-19; 11:1-4,15

JUNE 2

The Daily Bible **pages 694–698**

1 Kings 13:33-34; 14:1-18,22-24,30; 15:1-5;
2 Chronicles 11:5-12,18-23; 12:1-16; 13:1-22; 14:1

Key events, teaching, or concept:

Key verses:

What is God telling me about Himself or my relationship with Him?

How does this apply to my life today?

Parallel passages: 1 Kings 14:21,25-29,31; 15:6-8; 2 Chronicles 12:15

JUNE 3

The Daily Bible pages 698–704

1 Kings 14:19-20; 15:16-22,24-31,33-34; 16:1-29,31,34; 21:25-26; 22:41-44,46-47;
2 Chronicles 14:1–15:19; 16:7-14; 17:2–18:1; 20:32-33

Key events, teaching, or concept:

Key verses:

What is God telling me about Himself or my relationship with Him?

How does this apply to my life today?

Parallel passages: 1 Kings 15:8-15,23-24,32;
2 Chronicles 13:20; 16:1-6; 17:1; 18:1; 20:31

JUNE 4

The Daily Bible pages 704–709

1 Kings 17–19

Key events, teaching, or concept:

_____

_____

_____

_____

_____

Key verses:

_____

_____

_____

What is God telling me about Himself or my relationship with Him?

_____

_____

_____

_____

How does this apply to my life today?

_____

_____

_____

_____

The Daily Bible pages 709–715

1 Kings 20:1–21:24,27-29; 22:1-28; 2 Chronicles 18:2-3

Key events, teaching, or concept:

Key verses:

What is God telling me about Himself or my relationship with Him?

How does this apply to my life today?

Parallel passages: 2 Chronicles 18:4-27

JUNE 6

The Daily Bible pages 715–719

1 Kings 22:29-40,48-49,52-53; 2 Kings 1:2-18; 3:1-5;
2 Chronicles 19:1-11; 20:1-30,35-37

Key events, teaching, or concept:

Key verses:

What is God telling me about Himself or my relationship with Him?

How does this apply to my life today?

Parallel passages: 2 Chronicles 18:28-34

The Daily Bible pages 720–724

2 Kings 2:1-25; 4:1-44; 6:1-7; 8:1-2

Key events, teaching, or concept:

_____

_____

_____

_____

_____

Key verses:

_____

_____

_____

What is God telling me about Himself or my relationship with Him?

_____

_____

_____

_____

How does this apply to my life today?

_____

_____

_____

The Daily Bible pages 724–726

2 Kings 3:6-27; 8:16-17; 2 Chronicles 20:34; 21:1-4,6-17,20

Key events, teaching, or concept:

Key verses:

What is God telling me about Himself or my relationship with Him?

How does this apply to my life today?

Parallel passages: 1 Kings 22:45,50; 2 Kings 8:18-22; 2 Chronicles 21:5

JUNE 9

The Daily Bible pages 727–729

Obadiah

Key events, teaching, or concept:

Key verses:

What is God telling me about Himself or my relationship with Him?

How does this apply to my life today?

JUNE 10

The Daily Bible pages 729–734

2 Kings 5:1-27; 6:8–7:20; 8:3-6,8-23; 2 Chronicles 21:18

Key events, teaching, or concept:

Key verses:

What is God telling me about Himself or my relationship with Him?

How does this apply to my life today?

JUNE 11

The Daily Bible pages 734–738

2 Kings 8:7-15,23-26,28-29; 9:1-27,29-37; 10:1-17; 2 Chronicles 21:19-20; 22:1-4,7-9

Key events, teaching, or concept:

Key verses:

What is God telling me about Himself or my relationship with Him?

How does this apply to my life today?

Parallel passages: 2 Kings 8:27,29; 2 Chronicles 22:5-6

The Daily Bible pages 738–741

2 Kings 10:18-31; 11:13-16; 12:2-3; 2 Chronicles 22:10-12; 23:1-11,16-21

Key events, teaching, or concept:

Key verses:

What is God telling me about Himself or my relationship with Him?

How does this apply to my life today?

Parallel passages: 2 Kings 11:1-12,17-21; 12:1; 2 Chronicles 23:12-15; 24:1-2

The Daily Bible pages 741–748

Joel

Key events, teaching, or concept:

_____

_____

_____

_____

_____

Key verses:

_____

_____

_____

What is God telling me about Himself or my relationship with Him?

_____

_____

_____

_____

How does this apply to my life today?

_____

_____

_____

_____

JUNE 14

The Daily Bible pages 748–752

2 Kings 10:32-36; 12:4-21; 13:1-4,7-11,14-20;
2 Chronicles 24:3-27

Key events, teaching, or concept:

Key verses:

What is God telling me about Himself or my relationship with Him?

How does this apply to my life today?

The Daily Bible pages 752–755

2 Kings 12:21; 13:20-25; 14:1-6,15-16,23-24; 2 Chronicles 25:5-24

Key events, teaching, or concept:

_____

_____

_____

_____

_____

Key verses:

_____

_____

_____

What is God telling me about Himself or my relationship with Him?

_____

_____

_____

_____

How does this apply to my life today?

_____

_____

_____

Parallel passages: 2 Kings 13:12-13; 14: 7-14; 2 Chronicles 24:27; 25:1-4

JUNE 16

The Daily Bible pages 755–758

Jonah; 2 Kings 13:5-6; 14:25-27

Key events, teaching, or concept:

Key verses:

What is God telling me about Himself or my relationship with Him?

How does this apply to my life today?

JUNE 17

The Daily Bible pages 758–762

Hosea 1–3

Key events, teaching, or concept:

_____

_____

_____

_____

_____

Key verses:

_____

_____

_____

What is God telling me about Himself or my relationship with Him?

_____

_____

_____

_____

How does this apply to my life today?

_____

_____

_____

JUNE 18

The Daily Bible pages 762–769

Hosea 4–9

Key events, teaching, or concept:

Key verses:

What is God telling me about Himself or my relationship with Him?

How does this apply to my life today?

The Daily Bible pages 770–776

2 Kings 14:17,21; 15:1-2,3; 2 Chronicles 25:26-28; 26:1-15; Hosea 10–14

Key events, teaching, or concept:

Key verses:

What is God telling me about Himself or my relationship with Him?

How does this apply to my life today?

Parallel passages: 2 Kings 14:18-20,22; 15:3; 2 Chronicles 25:25

JUNE 20

The Daily Bible pages 776–782

Amos 1–4

Key events, teaching, or concept:

Key verses:

What is God telling me about Himself or my relationship with Him?

How does this apply to my life today?

The Daily Bible pages 782–788

Amos 5:1–7:9; 8–9

Key events, teaching, or concept:

_____

_____

_____

_____

_____

Key verses:

_____

_____

_____

What is God telling me about Himself or my relationship with Him?

_____

_____

_____

_____

How does this apply to my life today?

_____

_____

_____

_____

JUNE 22

The Daily Bible pages 788–790

Amos 7:10-17; 2 Kings 14:28-29; 15:8-18; 2 Chronicles 26:16-21

Key events, teaching, or concept:

Key verses:

What is God telling me about Himself or my relationship with Him?

How does this apply to my life today?

The Daily Bible pages 791–797

Isaiah 1:1-17,21-26; 2:6-18; 3:8–4:1; 5:1-25; 32:9-11

Key events, teaching, or concept:

Key verses:

What is God telling me about Himself or my relationship with Him?

How does this apply to my life today?

Parallel passages: 2 Kings 15:15

JUNE 24

The Daily Bible pages 798–803

2 Kings 15:7,19-28,32-33; 2 Chronicles 26:22-23; 27:2-6; Isaiah
1:18-20,27-31; 2:1-5,19–3:7; 4:2-6; 5:26-30; 6:1-13

Key events, teaching, or concept:

Key verses:

What is God telling me about Himself or my relationship with Him?

How does this apply to my life today?

Parallel passages: 2 Kings 15:6-7,34-35; 2 Chronicles 26:23; 27:1,8

JUNE 25

The Daily Bible pages 803–806

Micah 1–2

Key events, teaching, or concept:

_____

_____

_____

_____

_____

Key verses:

_____

_____

_____

What is God telling me about Himself or my relationship with Him?

_____

_____

_____

How does this apply to my life today?

_____

_____

_____

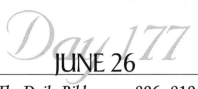

The Daily Bible pages 806–810

Micah 3–5

Key events, teaching, or concept:

Key verses:

What is God telling me about Himself or my relationship with Him?

How does this apply to my life today?

The Daily Bible pages 810–813

Micah 6–7

Key events, teaching, or concept:

_____

_____

_____

_____

_____

Key verses:

_____

_____

_____

What is God telling me about Himself or my relationship with Him?

_____

_____

_____

_____

How does this apply to my life today?

_____

_____

_____

_____

The Daily Bible pages 813–815

2 Kings 15:29-31,36-38; 16:1-2; 17:1-2;
1 Chronicles 5:23-26; 2 Chronicles 28:1-4

Key events, teaching, or concept:

Key verses:

What is God telling me about Himself or my relationship with Him?

How does this apply to my life today?

Parallel passages: 2 Kings 16:2-4; 2 Chronicles 27:7,9,28

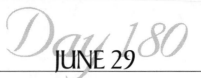

The Daily Bible pages 815–819

Isaiah 7–9

Key events, teaching, or concept:

_____

_____

_____

_____

_____

Key verses:

_____

_____

_____

What is God telling me about Himself or my relationship with Him?

_____

_____

_____

_____

How does this apply to my life today?

_____

_____

_____

_____

JUNE 30

The Daily Bible pages 819–825

Isaiah 10–12; 2 Chronicles 28:5-21

Key events, teaching, or concept:

_____

_____

_____

_____

_____

Key verses:

_____

_____

_____

What is God telling me about Himself or my relationship with Him?

_____

_____

_____

_____

How does this apply to my life today?

_____

_____

_____

Parallel passages: 2 Kings 16:5-6

JULY 1

The Daily Bible pages 825–829

Isaiah 14:24-27; 15–17; 34:1-4

Key events, teaching, or concept:

Key verses:

What is God telling me about Himself or my relationship with Him?

How does this apply to my life today?

The Daily Bible pages 829–833

Isaiah 21:11-17; 23; 34:5-17; 2 Kings 16:7-18,20; 18:1-7; 2 Chronicles 28:22-27

Key events, teaching, or concept:

Key verses:

What is God telling me about Himself or my relationship with Him?

How does this apply to my life today?

Parallel passages: 2 Kings 16:19-20; 2 Chronicles 28:27; 29:1-2

JULY 3

The Daily Bible pages 834–839

Isaiah 13–14; 21:1-10

Key events, teaching, or concept:

_____

_____

_____

_____

_____

Key verses:

_____

_____

_____

What is God telling me about Himself or my relationship with Him?

_____

_____

_____

_____

How does this apply to my life today?

_____

_____

_____

JULY 4

The Daily Bible pages 839–843

2 Chronicles 29:3–31:21

Key events, teaching, or concept:

_____

_____

_____

_____

_____

Key verses:

_____

_____

_____

What is God telling me about Himself or my relationship with Him?

_____

_____

_____

_____

How does this apply to my life today?

_____

_____

_____

The Daily Bible pages 844–849
Isaiah 24:1–25:9; 26:1–27:1; 32:1-8; 35

Key events, teaching, or concept:

_____

_____

_____

_____

Key verses:

_____

_____

_____

What is God telling me about Himself or my relationship with Him?

_____

_____

_____

How does this apply to my life today?

_____

_____

_____

JULY 6

Isaiah 22:1-14; 28:1–29:21; 33:1

Key events, teaching, or concept:

Key verses:

What is God telling me about Himself or my relationship with Him?

How does this apply to my life today?

JULY 7

The Daily Bible **pages 855–859**

Isaiah 22:15-25; 27:2-13; 29:22-24; 32:12-20; 33:2-24

Key events, teaching, or concept:

Key verses:

What is God telling me about Himself or my relationship with Him?

How does this apply to my life today?

JULY 8

The Daily Bible **pages 859–862**

2 Kings 17:3-5,7-41; 18:7-11

Key events, teaching, or concept:

Key verses:

What is God telling me about Himself or my relationship with Him?

How does this apply to my life today?

Parallel passages: 2 Kings 17:6; 18:12

The Daily Bible pages 863–869

Isaiah 18–20; 30–31

Key events, teaching, or concept:

_____

_____

_____

_____

Key verses:

_____

_____

_____

What is God telling me about Himself or my relationship with Him?

_____

_____

_____

How does this apply to my life today?

_____

_____

_____

JULY 10

The Daily Bible pages 870–877

2 Kings 18:13-37; 19:1-36; 20; 2 Chronicles 32:1-16,18-19,21-23,25-33
Isaiah 38:9-20

Key events, teaching, or concept:

Key verses:

What is God telling me about Himself or my relationship with Him?

How does this apply to my life today?

Parallel passages: 2 Chronicles 32:24; Isaiah 36:1-22; 37:1-37; 38:1-8,21,22; 39:1-8

The Daily Bible pages 877–878

2 Kings 20:21; 21:1-16

Key events, teaching, or concept:

Key verses:

What is God telling me about Himself or my relationship with Him?

How does this apply to my life today?

Parallel passages: 2 Chronicles 32:33; 33:1-9

JULY 12

The Daily Bible pages 878–883

Isaiah 40:1–41:10

Key events, teaching, or concept:

Key verses:

What is God telling me about Himself or my relationship with Him?

How does this apply to my life today?

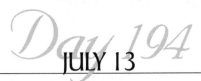

The Daily Bible pages 883–887

Isaiah 41:11–43:7

Key events, teaching, or concept:

_____

_____

_____

_____

_____

Key verses:

_____

_____

_____

What is God telling me about Himself or my relationship with Him?

_____

_____

_____

_____

How does this apply to my life today?

_____

_____

_____

JULY 14

The Daily Bible **pages 887–893**

Isaiah 43:8–45:13

Key events, teaching, or concept:

_____

_____

_____

_____

_____

Key verses:

_____

_____

_____

What is God telling me about Himself or my relationship with Him?

_____

_____

_____

How does this apply to my life today?

_____

_____

_____

_____

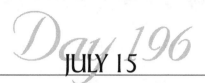

The Daily Bible pages 893–898

Isaiah 45:14–48:15

Key events, teaching, or concept:

_____

_____

_____

_____

_____

Key verses:

_____

_____

_____

What is God telling me about Himself or my relationship with Him?

_____

_____

_____

_____

How does this apply to my life today?

_____

_____

_____

The Daily Bible pages 898–902

Isaiah 48:16–50:11

Key events, teaching, or concept:

Key verses:

What is God telling me about Himself or my relationship with Him?

How does this apply to my life today?

The Daily Bible pages 902–907

Isaiah 51:1–54:3

Key events, teaching, or concept:

_____

_____

_____

_____

_____

Key verses:

_____

_____

_____

What is God telling me about Himself or my relationship with Him?

_____

_____

_____

How does this apply to my life today?

_____

_____

_____

JULY 18

The Daily Bible pages 908–911

Isaiah 54:4–56:12

Key events, teaching, or concept:

_____

_____

_____

_____

_____

Key verses:

_____

_____

What is God telling me about Himself or my relationship with Him?

_____

_____

_____

_____

How does this apply to my life today?

_____

_____

_____

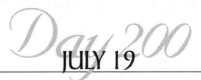

The Daily Bible pages 911–916

Isaiah 57–59

Key events, teaching, or concept:

_____

_____

_____

_____

_____

Key verses:

_____

_____

_____

What is God telling me about Himself or my relationship with Him?

_____

_____

_____

How does this apply to my life today?

_____

_____

_____

The Daily Bible pages 916–923

Isaiah 60–64

Key events, teaching, or concept:

Key verses:

What is God telling me about Himself or my relationship with Him?

How does this apply to my life today?

The Daily Bible pages 923–928

Isaiah 65–66

Key events, teaching, or concept:

_____

_____

_____

_____

_____

Key verses:

_____

_____

_____

What is God telling me about Himself or my relationship with Him?

_____

_____

_____

_____

How does this apply to my life today?

_____

_____

_____

JULY 22

The Daily Bible pages 929–933

2 Kings 19:37; 2 Chronicles 33:10-17; Nahum

Key events, teaching, or concept:

Key verses:

What is God telling me about Himself or my relationship with Him?

How does this apply to my life today?

Parallel passages: 2 Chronicles 32:21; Isaiah 37:38

JULY 23

The Daily Bible pages 934–935

2 Kings 21:17-19,23-26; 22:1-2; 23:25-27; 2 Chronicles 33:18-20,22-23

Key events, teaching, or concept:

_____
_____
_____
_____
_____

Key verses:

_____
_____
_____

What is God telling me about Himself or my relationship with Him?

_____
_____
_____
_____

How does this apply to my life today?

_____
_____
_____

Parallel passages: 2 Kings 21:20-22,26; 2 Chronicles 33:20-21,24-25; 34:1-2

The Daily Bible pages 935–941

Zephaniah

Key events, teaching, or concept:

Key verses:

What is God telling me about Himself or my relationship with Him?

How does this apply to my life today?

The Daily Bible **pages 941–947**

Jeremiah 1:1–3:5

Key events, teaching, or concept:

_____

_____

_____

_____

_____

Key verses:

_____

_____

_____

What is God telling me about Himself or my relationship with Him?

_____

_____

_____

_____

How does this apply to my life today?

_____

_____

_____

_____

The Daily Bible pages 947–953

Jeremiah 3:6–5:13

Key events, teaching, or concept:

_____

_____

_____

_____

_____

Key verses:

_____

_____

_____

What is God telling me about Himself or my relationship with Him?

_____

_____

_____

_____

How does this apply to my life today?

_____

_____

_____

_____

JULY 27

The Daily Bible pages 953–957

Jeremiah 5:14–6:30

Key events, teaching, or concept:

_____

_____

_____

_____

_____

Key verses:

_____

_____

_____

What is God telling me about Himself or my relationship with Him?

_____

_____

_____

_____

How does this apply to my life today?

_____

_____

_____

_____

JULY 28

The Daily Bible pages 957–963

Jeremiah 7–9

Key events, teaching, or concept:

_____

_____

_____

_____

Key verses:

_____

_____

_____

What is God telling me about Himself or my relationship with Him?

_____

_____

_____

_____

How does this apply to my life today?

_____

_____

_____

JULY 29

The Daily Bible pages 963–968

Jeremiah 10–12

Key events, teaching, or concept:

....

....

....

....

....

Key verses:

....

....

....

What is God telling me about Himself or my relationship with Him?

....

....

....

....

How does this apply to my life today?

....

....

....

....

JULY 30

The Daily Bible pages 968–973

Jeremiah 13:1–15:9

Key events, teaching, or concept:

Key verses:

What is God telling me about Himself or my relationship with Him?

How does this apply to my life today?

JULY 31

The Daily Bible pages 973–978

Jeremiah 15:10–17:18

Key events, teaching, or concept:

Key verses:

What is God telling me about Himself or my relationship with Him?

How does this apply to my life today?

AUGUST 1

The Daily Bible pages 978–983

Jeremiah 17:19–20:18

Key events, teaching, or concept:

_____

_____

_____

_____

_____

Key verses:

_____

_____

_____

What is God telling me about Himself or my relationship with Him?

_____

_____

_____

_____

How does this apply to my life today?

_____

_____

_____

AUGUST 2

The Daily Bible pages 983–987

2 Kings 22:3-8; 23:4-20,24; 2 Chronicles 34:8-33; 35:1-19,26-27

Key events, teaching, or concept:

Key verses:

What is God telling me about Himself or my relationship with Him?

How does this apply to my life today?

Parallel passages: 2 Kings 22:9-20; 23:1-3,21-23,28

AUGUST 3

The Daily Bible pages 987–991

2 Kings 23:30-37; 2 Chronicles 35:20-25; Jeremiah 22:10-17; 26

Key events, teaching, or concept:

Key verses:

What is God telling me about Himself or my relationship with Him?

How does this apply to my life today?

Parallel passages: 2 Kings 23:29-30; 2 Chronicles 36:1-6

The Daily Bible pages 991–994

Jeremiah 46–47

Key events, teaching, or concept:

_____

_____

_____

_____

_____

Key verses:

_____

_____

_____

What is God telling me about Himself or my relationship with Him?

_____

_____

_____

_____

How does this apply to my life today?

_____

_____

_____

_____

AUGUST 5

The Daily Bible pages 994–999

Habakkuk

Key events, teaching, or concept:

_____

_____

_____

_____

_____

Key verses:

_____

_____

_____

What is God telling me about Himself or my relationship with Him?

_____

_____

_____

_____

How does this apply to my life today?

_____

_____

_____

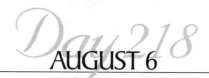

AUGUST 6

The Daily Bible **pages 999–1003**

2 Kings 24:1,7; 2 Chronicles 36:6-7; Jeremiah 25; 35

Key events, teaching, or concept:

_____

_____

_____

_____

_____

Key verses:

_____

_____

_____

What is God telling me about Himself or my relationship with Him?

_____

_____

_____

_____

How does this apply to my life today?

_____

_____

_____

_____

AUGUST 7

The Daily Bible pages 1003–1005

Jeremiah 36; 45

Key events, teaching, or concept:

_____

_____

_____

_____

_____

Key verses:

_____

_____

_____

What is God telling me about Himself or my relationship with Him?

_____

_____

_____

_____

How does this apply to my life today?

_____

_____

_____

AUGUST 8

The Daily Bible pages 1006–1010

Daniel 1:3-20; 2

Key events, teaching, or concept:

Key verses:

What is God telling me about Himself or my relationship with Him?

How does this apply to my life today?

AUGUST 9

The Daily Bible pages 1010–1018

2 Kings 24:1-4; Jeremiah 22:18-23; 24:5-6; 48:1–49:33

Key events, teaching, or concept:

_____

_____

_____

_____

_____

Key verses:

_____

_____

_____

What is God telling me about Himself or my relationship with Him?

_____

_____

_____

_____

How does this apply to my life today?

_____

_____

_____

AUGUST 10

The Daily Bible pages 1018–1020

2 Kings 24:6,8-20; 2 Chronicles 36:10,12,13-16;
Jeremiah 22:24-30; 37:1-2; Daniel 1:2

Key events, teaching, or concept:

Key verses:

What is God telling me about Himself or my relationship with Him?

How does this apply to my life today?

Parallel passages: 2 Chronicles 36:8-11; Daniel 1:1; Jeremiah 52:1-3

AUGUST 11

The Daily Bible pages 1020–1024

Jeremiah 24; 27–29

Key events, teaching, or concept:

Key verses:

What is God telling me about Himself or my relationship with Him?

How does this apply to my life today?

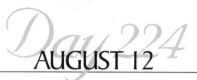

AUGUST 12

The Daily Bible pages 1024–1026

Jeremiah 23:9-40

Key events, teaching, or concept:

_____

_____

_____

_____

_____

Key verses:

_____

_____

_____

What is God telling me about Himself or my relationship with Him?

_____

_____

_____

_____

How does this apply to my life today?

_____

_____

_____

_____

The Daily Bible pages 1026–1030

Jeremiah 50:1-40; 51:59

Key events, teaching, or concept:

Key verses:

What is God telling me about Himself or my relationship with Him?

How does this apply to my life today?

AUGUST 14

The Daily Bible pages 1030–1038

Jeremiah 34:8-22; 49:34-39; 50:41-46; 51

Key events, teaching, or concept:

_____

_____

_____

_____

_____

Key verses:

_____

_____

_____

What is God telling me about Himself or my relationship with Him?

_____

_____

_____

_____

How does this apply to my life today?

_____

_____

_____

The Daily Bible pages 1038–1045

Ezekiel 1–7

Key events, teaching, or concept:

Key verses:

What is God telling me about Himself or my relationship with Him?

How does this apply to my life today?

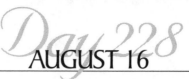

The Daily Bible pages 1045–1049

Ezekiel 8–11

Key events, teaching, or concept:

_____

_____

_____

_____

_____

Key verses:

_____

_____

_____

What is God telling me about Himself or my relationship with Him?

_____

_____

_____

How does this apply to my life today?

_____

_____

_____

The Daily Bible pages 1049–1053

Ezekiel 12–14

Key events, teaching, or concept:

Key verses:

What is God telling me about Himself or my relationship with Him?

How does this apply to my life today?

The Daily Bible pages 1053–1060

Ezekiel 15–18

Key events, teaching, or concept:

Key verses:

What is God telling me about Himself or my relationship with Him?

How does this apply to my life today?

AUGUST 19

The Daily Bible pages 1060–1067

Ezekiel 19–21

Key events, teaching, or concept:

_____

_____

_____

_____

Key verses:

_____

_____

What is God telling me about Himself or my relationship with Him?

_____

_____

_____

How does this apply to my life today?

_____

_____

_____

The Daily Bible pages 1067–1070

2 Kings 25:1; 2 Chronicles 36:13; Jeremiah 52:4; Ezekiel 23

Key events, teaching, or concept:

Key verses:

What is God telling me about Himself or my relationship with Him?

How does this apply to my life today?

Parallel passages: 2 Kings 24:20; Jeremiah 39:1; 52:3

AUGUST 21

The Daily Bible pages 1070–1072

Ezekiel 24

Key events, teaching, or concept:

Key verses:

What is God telling me about Himself or my relationship with Him?

How does this apply to my life today?

AUGUST 22

The Daily Bible **pages 1072–1077**

Jeremiah 21:1–22:9; 32:1–33:9; 34:1-7

Key events, teaching, or concept:

_____

_____

_____

_____

_____

Key verses:

_____

_____

_____

What is God telling me about Himself or my relationship with Him?

_____

_____

_____

_____

How does this apply to my life today?

_____

_____

_____

_____

AUGUST 23

The Daily Bible pages 1077–1082

Jeremiah 30:1–31:26; 33:10-13

Key events, teaching, or concept:

Key verses:

What is God telling me about Himself or my relationship with Him?

How does this apply to my life today?

AUGUST 24

The Daily Bible pages 1082–1085

Jeremiah 23:1-8; 31:27-40; 33:14-26

Key events, teaching, or concept:

_____

_____

_____

_____

_____

Key verses:

_____

_____

_____

What is God telling me about Himself or my relationship with Him?

_____

_____

_____

_____

How does this apply to my life today?

_____

_____

_____

_____

The Daily Bible pages 1085–1091

Ezekiel 25:1-17; 29:1-16; 30–31

Key events, teaching, or concept:

_____

_____

_____

_____

_____

Key verses:

_____

_____

_____

What is God telling me about Himself or my relationship with Him?

_____

_____

_____

_____

How does this apply to my life today?

_____

_____

_____

_____

AUGUST 26

The Daily Bible pages 1091–1096

Ezekiel 26–28

Key events, teaching, or concept:

_____

_____

_____

_____

_____

Key verses:

_____

_____

_____

What is God telling me about Himself or my relationship with Him?

_____

_____

_____

_____

How does this apply to my life today?

_____

_____

_____

_____

AUGUST 27

The Daily Bible pages 1097–1099

Jeremiah 27:17-21; 38

Key events, teaching, or concept:

Key verses:

What is God telling me about Himself or my relationship with Him?

How does this apply to my life today?

The Daily Bible pages 1100–1103

2 Kings 25:2-4,22; 2 Chronicles 36:17,19-21;
Jeremiah 39:2-5,9-18; 40:1-6; 52:9-23,27-30

Key events, teaching, or concept:

_____

_____

_____

_____

_____

Key verses:

_____

_____

_____

What is God telling me about Himself or my relationship with Him?

_____

_____

_____

_____

How does this apply to my life today?

_____

_____

_____

_____

Parallel passages: 2 Kings 25:4-21; 2 Chronicles 36:18;
Jeremiah 39:5-8; 52:5-9,24-27

AUGUST 29

The Daily Bible pages 1103–1109

Lamentations 1–2

Key events, teaching, or concept:

_____

_____

_____

_____

Key verses:

_____

_____

_____

What is God telling me about Himself or my relationship with Him?

_____

_____

_____

How does this apply to my life today?

_____

_____

_____

The Daily Bible pages 1109–1115

Lamentations 3–5

Key events, teaching, or concept:

_____

_____

_____

_____

_____

Key verses:

_____

_____

_____

What is God telling me about Himself or my relationship with Him?

_____

_____

_____

_____

How does this apply to my life today?

_____

_____

_____

_____

AUGUST 31

The Daily Bible pages 1115–1120

Jeremiah 40:7-16; 41–44; 51:64

Key events, teaching, or concept:

Key verses:

What is God telling me about Himself or my relationship with Him?

How does this apply to my life today?

Parallel passages 2 Kings 25:23-26

SEPTEMBER 1

The Daily Bible **pages 1121–1126**

Ezekiel 33:21-33; 34–36

Key events, teaching, or concept:

_____

_____

_____

_____

_____

Key verses:

_____

_____

_____

What is God telling me about Himself or my relationship with Him?

_____

_____

_____

_____

How does this apply to my life today?

_____

_____

_____

SEPTEMBER 2

The Daily Bible pages 1126–1130

Ezekiel 37–39

Key events, teaching, or concept:

_____

_____

_____

_____

_____

Key verses:

_____

_____

_____

What is God telling me about Himself or my relationship with Him?

_____

_____

_____

_____

How does this apply to my life today?

_____

_____

_____

The Daily Bible pages 1130–1134

Ezekiel 32

Key events, teaching, or concept:

_____

_____

_____

_____

_____

Key verses:

_____

_____

_____

What is God telling me about Himself or my relationship with Him?

_____

_____

_____

_____

How does this apply to my life today?

_____

_____

_____

SEPTEMBER 4

The Daily Bible pages 1134–1136

Daniel 3

Key events, teaching, or concept:

Key verses:

What is God telling me about Himself or my relationship with Him?

How does this apply to my life today?

SEPTEMBER 5

The Daily Bible pages 1136–1143

Ezekiel 40–43; 44:1-3

Key events, teaching, or concept:

_____

_____

_____

_____

Key verses:

_____

_____

_____

What is God telling me about Himself or my relationship with Him?

_____

_____

_____

_____

How does this apply to my life today?

_____

_____

_____

SEPTEMBER 6

The Daily Bible pages 1143–1150

Ezekiel 44:4–48:35

Key events, teaching, or concept:

Key verses:

What is God telling me about Himself or my relationship with Him?

How does this apply to my life today?

SEPTEMBER 7

The Daily Bible pages 1150–1154

Ezekiel 29:17-21; Daniel 4

Key events, teaching, or concept:

Key verses:

What is God telling me about Himself or my relationship with Him?

How does this apply to my life today?

SEPTEMBER 8

The Daily Bible pages 1155–1159

Job 1–3

Key events, teaching, or concept:

Key verses:

What is God telling me about Himself or my relationship with Him?

How does this apply to my life today?

SEPTEMBER 9

The Daily Bible pages 1159–1164

Job 4–7

Key events, teaching, or concept:

Key verses:

What is God telling me about Himself or my relationship with Him?

How does this apply to my life today?

SEPTEMBER 10

The Daily Bible pages 1164–1168

Job 8–10

Key events, teaching, or concept:

Key verses:

What is God telling me about Himself or my relationship with Him?

How does this apply to my life today?

Key events, teaching, or concept:

Key verses:

What is God telling me about Himself or my relationship with Him?

How does this apply to my life today?

SEPTEMBER 12

The Daily Bible pages 1173–1176

Job 15–17

Key events, teaching, or concept:

_____

_____

_____

_____

_____

Key verses:

_____

_____

_____

What is God telling me about Himself or my relationship with Him?

_____

_____

_____

_____

How does this apply to my life today?

_____

_____

_____

The Daily Bible pages 1176–1182

Job 18–21

Key events, teaching, or concept:

_____

_____

_____

_____

_____

Key verses:

_____

_____

_____

What is God telling me about Himself or my relationship with Him?

_____

_____

_____

_____

How does this apply to my life today?

_____

_____

_____

_____

SEPTEMBER 14

The Daily Bible pages 1182–1185

Job 22–24

Key events, teaching, or concept:

Key verses:

What is God telling me about Himself or my relationship with Him?

How does this apply to my life today?

SEPTEMBER 15

The Daily Bible **pages 1185–1193**

Job 25–31

Key events, teaching, or concept:

Key verses:

What is God telling me about Himself or my relationship with Him?

How does this apply to my life today?

SEPTEMBER 16

The Daily Bible pages 1193–1202

Job 32–37

Key events, teaching, or concept:

Key verses:

What is God telling me about Himself or my relationship with Him?

How does this apply to my life today?

SEPTEMBER 17

The Daily Bible **pages 1202–1209**

Job 38–42

Key events, teaching, or concept:

_____

_____

_____

_____

_____

Key verses:

_____

_____

_____

What is God telling me about Himself or my relationship with Him?

_____

_____

_____

_____

How does this apply to my life today?

_____

_____

_____

SEPTEMBER 18

The Daily Bible pages 1209–1217

Psalm 44; 74; 79–80; 85; 89

Key events, teaching, or concept:

Key verses:

What is God telling me about Himself or my relationship with Him?

How does this apply to my life today?

The Daily Bible pages 1217–1221

Psalm 102; 106; 123; 137

Key events, teaching, or concept:

_____

_____

_____

_____

Key verses:

_____

_____

_____

What is God telling me about Himself or my relationship with Him?

_____

_____

_____

How does this apply to my life today?

_____

_____

_____

SEPTEMBER 20

The Daily Bible pages 1221–1225

Daniel 7–8

Key events, teaching, or concept:

Key verses:

What is God telling me about Himself or my relationship with Him?

How does this apply to my life today?

The Daily Bible pages 1225–1229

Daniel 5; 9

Key events, teaching, or concept:

_____

_____

_____

_____

_____

Key verses:

_____

_____

_____

What is God telling me about Himself or my relationship with Him?

_____

_____

_____

How does this apply to my life today?

_____

_____

_____

SEPTEMBER 22

The Daily Bible pages 1230–1232

Daniel 1:21; 6

Key events, teaching, or concept:

Key verses:

What is God telling me about Himself or my relationship with Him?

How does this apply to my life today?

SEPTEMBER 23

The Daily Bible pages 1233–1238

Ezra 2:64–4:5

Key events, teaching, or concept:

Key verses:

What is God telling me about Himself or my relationship with Him?

How does this apply to my life today?

SEPTEMBER 24

The Daily Bible pages 1238–1242

Daniel 10–12

Key events, teaching, or concept:

_____

_____

_____

_____

_____

Key verses:

_____

_____

_____

What is God telling me about Himself or my relationship with Him?

_____

_____

_____

_____

How does this apply to my life today?

_____

_____

_____

_____

SEPTEMBER 25

The Daily Bible pages 1243–1246

Ezra 4:6-24; 5:1–6:13

Key events, teaching, or concept:

_____

_____

_____

_____

_____

Key verses:

_____

_____

_____

What is God telling me about Himself or my relationship with Him?

_____

_____

_____

_____

How does this apply to my life today?

_____

_____

_____

SEPTEMBER 26

The Daily Bible pages 1247–1250

Haggai; Zechariah 1:1-6

Key events, teaching, or concept:

Key verses:

What is God telling me about Himself or my relationship with Him?

How does this apply to my life today?

SEPTEMBER 27

The Daily Bible pages 1250–1254

Zechariah 1:7–6:15

Key events, teaching, or concept:

_____

_____

_____

_____

_____

Key verses:

_____

_____

_____

What is God telling me about Himself or my relationship with Him?

_____

_____

_____

_____

How does this apply to my life today?

_____

_____

_____

SEPTEMBER 28

The Daily Bible **pages 1255–1257**

Ezra 6:14-22; Zechariah 7–8

Key events, teaching, or concept:

Key verses:

What is God telling me about Himself or my relationship with Him?

How does this apply to my life today?

SEPTEMBER 29

The Daily Bible pages 1258–1261

Psalm 78

Key events, teaching, or concept:

_____

_____

_____

_____

_____

Key verses:

_____

_____

_____

What is God telling me about Himself or my relationship with Him?

_____

_____

_____

How does this apply to my life today?

_____

_____

_____

SEPTEMBER 30

The Daily Bible **pages 1261–1266**

Psalm 107; 116; 118; 125

Key events, teaching, or concept:

_____

_____

_____

_____

_____

Key verses:

_____

_____

_____

What is God telling me about Himself or my relationship with Him?

_____

_____

_____

_____

How does this apply to my life today?

_____

_____

_____

_____

OCTOBER 1

Key events, teaching, or concept:

_____

_____

_____

_____

_____

Key verses:

_____

_____

_____

What is God telling me about Himself or my relationship with Him?

_____

_____

_____

How does this apply to my life today?

_____

_____

_____

OCTOBER 2

The Daily Bible pages 1269–1276

Zechariah 9–14

Key events, teaching, or concept:

Key verses:

What is God telling me about Himself or my relationship with Him?

How does this apply to my life today?

OCTOBER 3

The Daily Bible pages 1276–1280

Esther 1–4

Key events, teaching, or concept:

Key verses:

What is God telling me about Himself or my relationship with Him?

How does this apply to my life today?

OCTOBER 4

The Daily Bible **pages 1281–1285**

Esther 5–10

Key events, teaching, or concept:

_____

_____

_____

_____

_____

Key verses:

_____

_____

_____

What is God telling me about Himself or my relationship with Him?

_____

_____

_____

_____

How does this apply to my life today?

_____

_____

_____

The Daily Bible pages 1286–1290

Malachi

Key events, teaching, or concept:

_____

_____

_____

_____

_____

Key verses:

_____

_____

_____

What is God telling me about Himself or my relationship with Him?

_____

_____

_____

_____

How does this apply to my life today?

_____

_____

_____

_____

OCTOBER 6

The Daily Bible **pages 1290–1293**

Ezra 7–8

Key events, teaching, or concept:

Key verses:

What is God telling me about Himself or my relationship with Him?

How does this apply to my life today?

The Daily Bible pages 1293–1296

Ezra 9–10

Key events, teaching, or concept:

_____

_____

_____

_____

_____

Key verses:

_____

_____

_____

What is God telling me about Himself or my relationship with Him?

_____

_____

_____

_____

How does this apply to my life today?

_____

_____

_____

The Daily Bible pages 1297–1300

Nehemiah 1–3

Key events, teaching, or concept:

Key verses:

What is God telling me about Himself or my relationship with Him?

How does this apply to my life today?

OCTOBER 9

The Daily Bible pages 1300–1304

Nehemiah 4–6

Key events, teaching, or concept:

Key verses:

What is God telling me about Himself or my relationship with Him?

How does this apply to my life today?

OCTOBER 10

The Daily Bible pages 1304–1309

Nehemiah 7; 11:1–12:26

Key events, teaching, or concept:

Key verses:

What is God telling me about Himself or my relationship with Him?

How does this apply to my life today?

OCTOBER 11

The Daily Bible pages 1309–1314

Nehemiah 8–10

Key events, teaching, or concept:

_____

_____

_____

_____

_____

Key verses:

_____

_____

_____

What is God telling me about Himself or my relationship with Him?

_____

_____

_____

How does this apply to my life today?

_____

_____

_____

OCTOBER 12

The Daily Bible pages 1315–1318

Nehemiah 12:27–13:31

Key events, teaching, or concept:

_____

_____

_____

_____

Key verses:

_____

_____

_____

What is God telling me about Himself or my relationship with Him?

_____

_____

_____

_____

How does this apply to my life today?

_____

_____

_____

The Daily Bible pages 1318–1326

1 Chronicles 1–2; 3:10–4:23

Key events, teaching, or concept:

Key verses:

What is God telling me about Himself or my relationship with Him?

How does this apply to my life today?

OCTOBER 14

The Daily Bible pages 1326–1336
1 Chronicles 4:24–5:17; 6:1–9:34

Key events, teaching, or concept:

Key verses:

What is God telling me about Himself or my relationship with Him?

How does this apply to my life today?

The Daily Bible pages 1337–1339

(See "End of the Old Testament Record.")

What are the most powerful lessons I remember from the Old Testament?

_____

_____

_____

_____

What Old Testament passages or verses stand out most clearly?

_____

_____

_____

What do God's dealings with mankind from Creation onward tell me about my relationship with Him?

_____

_____

_____

_____

How does God's interaction with the nation of Israel apply to my life today?

_____

_____

_____

OCTOBER 16

The Daily Bible pages 1339–1343

(See "Writings of the Apocrypha.")

From these brief summaries of the Apocrypha, what seem to be the main concerns during the period between the Testaments?

Which of these writings has the most appeal for further reading?

Does this brief introduction point to any message about my relationship with God?

How do interludes of silence and anticipation in my own life affect me today?

OCTOBER 17

The Daily Bible pages 1343–1348

(See "Influences on a Dispersed People," "Hellenism and
the Jews," and "Judaism Under Roman Rule.")

In what way has God worked through history to prepare the way for
fresh beginnings?

_____

_____

_____

_____

Which of the events in the four centuries before Christ seem to be the
most important to the coming Kingdom?

_____

_____

_____

What do the political changes leading to the birth of Christ teach me
about my relationship with God?

_____

_____

_____

How does this period of ancient history apply to my life today?

_____

_____

_____

OCTOBER 18

The Daily Bible **pages 1349–1352**

Mark 1:1; Luke 1:1-4; John 1:1-18

Key events, teaching, or concept:

Key verses:

What is God telling me about Himself or my relationship with Him?

How does this apply to my life today?

OCTOBER 19

The Daily Bible **pages 1353–1355**

Matthew 1:1-17; Luke 3:23-38

Key events, teaching, or concept:

Key verses:

What is God telling me about Himself or my relationship with Him?

How does this apply to my life today?

OCTOBER 20

The Daily Bible pages 1355–1361

Matthew 1:18-25; Luke 1:5-80; 2:1-38

Key events, teaching, or concept:

_____

_____

_____

_____

_____

Key verses:

_____

_____

_____

What is God telling me about Himself or my relationship with Him?

_____

_____

_____

_____

How does this apply to my life today?

_____

_____

_____

OCTOBER 21

The Daily Bible **pages 1361–1363**

Matthew 2:1-23; Luke 2:39-52

Key events, teaching, or concept:

Key verses:

What is God telling me about Himself or my relationship with Him?

How does this apply to my life today?

OCTOBER 22

The Daily Bible pages 1364–1367

Matthew 3:4-6,13-17; 4:1-11; Luke 3:1-6,15-18,21-23; John 1:19-34

Key events, teaching, or concept:

Key verses:

What is God telling me about Himself or my relationship with Him?

How does this apply to my life today?

Parallel passages: Matthew 3:1-3,7-12; Mark 1:2-4,7-13; Luke 4:1-13

OCTOBER 23

The Daily Bible pages 1367–1373

Luke 3:19-20; John 1:35-51; 2–4

Key events, teaching, or concept:

_____

_____

_____

_____

Key verses:

_____

_____

_____

What is God telling me about Himself or my relationship with Him?

_____

_____

_____

How does this apply to my life today?

_____

_____

_____

OCTOBER 24

The Daily Bible pages 1373–1376

Matthew 4:12-25; Mark 1:21-45; 2:1-12; Luke 4:14-30; 5:1-11,21-28

Key events, teaching, or concept:

Key verses:

What is God telling me about Himself or my relationship with Him?

How does this apply to my life today?

Parallel passages: Matthew 8:1-4,14-17; 9:1-8; Mark 1:14-20; Luke 4:31-44; 5:12-26

OCTOBER 25

The Daily Bible pages 1376–1380

Matthew 9:10-13; 12:1-21; Mark 2:13-14,23-28; 3:1-12;
Luke 5:29-39; 6:6-19; John 5:1-3,5-47

Key events, teaching, or concept:

_____

_____

_____

_____

_____

Key verses:

_____

_____

_____

What is God telling me about Himself or my relationship with Him?

_____

_____

_____

_____

How does this apply to my life today?

_____

_____

_____

_____

Parallel passages: Matthew 9:9,14-17; Mark 2:15-22; 3:13-19; Luke 5:27-28; 6:1-5

OCTOBER 26

The Daily Bible pages 1381–1386

Matthew 5:1-48; 6:1-34; 7:6-29; Luke 6:24-49

Key events, teaching, or concept:

_____

_____

_____

_____

Key verses:

_____

_____

What is God telling me about Himself or my relationship with Him?

_____

_____

_____

_____

How does this apply to my life today?

_____

_____

_____

_____

Parallel passages: Matthew 7:1-5; Luke 6:20-23

OCTOBER 27

The Daily Bible pages 1386–1390

Matthew 8:5-13; 11:7-15; 12:22-42; Mark 3:20-30; Luke 7:1–8:3

Key events, teaching, or concept:

Key verses:

What is God telling me about Himself or my relationship with Him?

How does this apply to my life today?

Parallel passages: Matthew 11:2-6,16-19; Luke 11:14-23,29-32

OCTOBER 28

The Daily Bible pages 1390–1394

Luke 11:37–13:17

Key events, teaching, or concept:

Key verses:

What is God telling me about Himself or my relationship with Him?

How does this apply to my life today?

OCTOBER 29

The Daily Bible pages 1394–1397

Matthew 13:1-52; Mark 4:21-29,33-34

Key events, teaching, or concept:

_____

_____

_____

_____

_____

Key verses:

_____

_____

_____

What is God telling me about Himself or my relationship with Him?

_____

_____

_____

_____

How does this apply to my life today?

_____

_____

_____

_____

Parallel passages: Mark 4:1-20,30-32; Luke 8:4-18; 13:18-21

OCTOBER 30

The Daily Bible pages 1397–1400

Matthew 8:18-22; 9:27-34; Mark 4:35–6:6; Luke 9:57-62

Key events, teaching, or concept:

Key verses:

What is God telling me about Himself or my relationship with Him?

How does this apply to my life today?

Parallel passages: Matthew 8:23-34; 9:18-26; 13:53-58; Luke 8:22-56

OCTOBER 31

The Daily Bible **pages 1400–1403**

Matthew 9:35-38; 10:1–11:1; 14:3-12; Mark 6:7,14-33; Luke 9:11; John 6:1

Key events, teaching, or concept:

Key verses:

What is God telling me about Himself or my relationship with Him?

How does this apply to my life today?

Parallel passages: Matthew 14:1-2,12-13; Mark 6:6,8-13; Luke 9:1-5

NOVEMBER 1

The Daily Bible pages 1403–1408

Matthew 14:28-33; 15:10-20; Mark 6:34-56; 7:1-23; Luke 9:11; John 6:5–7:1

Key events, teaching, or concept:

_____

_____

_____

_____

_____

Key verses:

_____

_____

_____

What is God telling me about Himself or my relationship with Him?

_____

_____

_____

_____

How does this apply to my life today?

_____

_____

_____

_____

Parallel passages: Matthew 14:14-27,34-36; 15:1-9; Luke 9:12-17; John 6:2-4

NOVEMBER 2

The Daily Bible pages 1408–1410

Matthew 15:21-31; 16:1-12; Mark 7:24–8:26

Key events, teaching, or concept:

_____

_____

_____

_____

_____

Key verses:

_____

_____

_____

What is God telling me about Himself or my relationship with Him?

_____

_____

_____

_____

How does this apply to my life today?

_____

_____

_____

_____

Parallel passages: Matthew 15:32-39

NOVEMBER 3

The Daily Bible pages 1410–1415

Matthew 16:13-23; 17:1-21,24-27; 18:1-35;
Mark 8:34–9:1,14-45; Luke 9:46-48; 17:3-4,7-10

Key events, teaching, or concept:

_____

_____

_____

_____

_____

Key verses:

_____

_____

_____

What is God telling me about Himself or my relationship with Him?

_____

_____

_____

_____

How does this apply to my life today?

_____

_____

_____

_____

Parallel passages: Matthew 16:24-28; 17:22-23; Mark
8:27-33; 9:2-13; Luke 9:18-45,49-50; 17:1-3,5-6

NOVEMBER 4

The Daily Bible pages 1415–1418

John 7:2–8:11

Key events, teaching, or concept:

_____

_____

_____

_____

_____

Key verses:

_____

_____

_____

What is God telling me about Himself or my relationship with Him?

_____

_____

_____

_____

How does this apply to my life today?

_____

_____

_____

_____

NOVEMBER 5

The Daily Bible pages 1418–1422

John 8:12–10:21

Key events, teaching, or concept:

Key verses:

What is God telling me about Himself or my relationship with Him?

How does this apply to my life today?

NOVEMBER 6

The Daily Bible pages 1422–1426

Matthew 11:28-30; Luke 9:51-56; 10:1-42; 11:1-13; 17:11-19;
John 10:22-42

Key events, teaching, or concept:

Key verses:

What is God telling me about Himself or my relationship with Him?

How does this apply to my life today?

Parallel passages: Matthew 11:20-27; 19:1-2; Mark 10:1

NOVEMBER 7

The Daily Bible pages 1427–1433

Matthew 20:1-6; Luke 13:22–16:31; 17:20-35,37; 18:1-14

Key events, teaching, or concept:

_____

_____

_____

_____

_____

Key verses:

_____

_____

_____

What is God telling me about Himself or my relationship with Him?

_____

_____

_____

_____

How does this apply to my life today?

_____

_____

_____

NOVEMBER 8

The Daily Bible pages 1433–1435

John 11:1-54

Key events, teaching, or concept:

Key verses:

What is God telling me about Himself or my relationship with Him?

How does this apply to my life today?

NOVEMBER 9

The Daily Bible pages 1435–1440

Matthew 19:3-12,27-30; 20:20-23; 26:6-13; Mark 10:10-27,32-52;
14:3-9; Luke 18:31–19:28; John 11:55-57; 12:1-11

Key events, teaching, or concept:

_____

_____

_____

_____

_____

Key verses:

_____

_____

_____

What is God telling me about Himself or my relationship with Him?

_____

_____

_____

_____

How does this apply to my life today?

_____

_____

_____

Parallel passages: Matthew 19:13-26; 20:17-19,24-34;
Mark 10:2-9,28-31; Luke 18:15-30

NOVEMBER 10

The Daily Bible pages 1440–1443

Matthew 21:1-7,10-11,14-16; Mark 11:1-19; Luke 19:29-44,47-48; John 12:12-36

Key events, teaching, or concept:

Key verses:

What is God telling me about Himself or my relationship with Him?

How does this apply to my life today?

Parallel passages: Matthew 21:8-9,12-13,17-19; Luke 19:45-46

NOVEMBER 11

The Daily Bible pages 1443–1449

Matthew 21:20-22,28-32,42-46; 22:1-33,41-46; 23:1-39;
Mark 11:20-33; 12:1-9,28-37,41-44; Luke 20:9-16,20-26

Key events, teaching, or concept:

Key verses:

What is God telling me about Himself or my relationship with Him?

How does this apply to my life today?

Parallel passages: Matthew 21:23-27,33-41; 22:34-40; Mark
12:10-27,38-40; Luke 20:1-8,17-19,27-28,39-47; 21:1-4

The Daily Bible **pages 1449–1453**

Matthew 24:3-51; 25:1-46; Mark 13:1-31,34-37; Luke 21:8-36

Key events, teaching, or concept:

Key verses:

What is God telling me about Himself or my relationship with Him?

How does this apply to my life today?

Parallel passages: Matthew 24:1-3; Mark 13:32-33; Luke 21:5-7

NOVEMBER 13

The Daily Bible pages 1453–1457

Matthew 26:1-5,14-16; Luke 21:37-38; 22:3-13; John 12:37-50

Key events, teaching, or concept:

Key verses:

What is God telling me about Himself or my relationship with Him?

How does this apply to my life today?

Parallel passages: Matthew 26:17-19; Mark 14:1-2,10-16; Luke 22:1-2

NOVEMBER 14

The Daily Bible pages 1457–1461

Matthew 26:22-25,30-35; Luke 22:14-21,23-38; John 13–14

Key events, teaching, or concept:

Key verses:

What is God telling me about Himself or my relationship with Him?

How does this apply to my life today?

Parallel passages: Matthew 26:20-21,26-29; Mark 14:17-31; Luke 22:22,39

NOVEMBER 15

The Daily Bible **pages 1462–1465**

John 15–17

Key events, teaching, or concept:

_____

_____

_____

_____

_____

Key verses:

_____

_____

_____

What is God telling me about Himself or my relationship with Him?

_____

_____

_____

_____

How does this apply to my life today?

_____

_____

_____

_____

NOVEMBER 16

The Daily Bible pages 1465–1469

Matthew 26:40-46,50-54,56,69-74; 27:1,3-10; Mark 14:32-34,37-39,
43-47,50-52,55-64; Luke 22:41-71; John 18:1-27

Key events, teaching, or concept:

_____

_____

_____

_____

_____

Key verses:

_____

_____

_____

What is God telling me about Himself or my relationship with Him?

_____

_____

_____

_____

How does this apply to my life today?

_____

_____

_____

Parallel passages: Matthew 26:36-39,47-50,55-68,74-75;
Mark 14:35-36,40-42,48-49,53-54,65-72; 15:1; Luke 22:40

The Daily Bible pages 1470–1473

Matthew 27:2,11-14,19-25,27-31; Mark 15:6-11,20-22;
Luke 23:1-2,5-16,18-25,27-31; John 18:28-38,40; 19:1-17

Key events, teaching, or concept:

Key verses:

What is God telling me about Himself or my relationship with Him?

How does this apply to my life today?

Parallel passages: Matthew 27:15-18,26,32; Mark
15:1-5,12-19; Luke 23:3-12,26; John 18:39

NOVEMBER 18

The Daily Bible pages 1473–1477

Matthew 27:39-49,51-56,59-60,62-66; Mark 5:23,25,27-28;15:39-45;
Luke 23:32-37,39-43,46-49,55-56; John 19:19-42

Key events, teaching, or concept:

Key verses:

What is God telling me about Himself or my relationship with Him?

How does this apply to my life today?

NOVEMBER 19

The Daily Bible pages 1477–1484

Matthew 28:2-4,8-20; Mark 16:1-9,15-18,20; Luke 24:4-11,
13-53; John 20:2-19,21-31; 21; Acts 1:6-26

Key events, teaching, or concept:

Key verses:

What is God telling me about Himself or my relationship with Him?

How does this apply to my life today?

Parallel passages: Matthew 28:1,5-7; Mark 16:10-14,19; Luke 24:1-3,12; John 20:1,20

NOVEMBER 20

The Daily Bible **pages 1485–1488**

Acts 1:1-5; 2

Key events, teaching, or concept:

_____

_____

_____

_____

_____

Key verses:

_____

_____

_____

What is God telling me about Himself or my relationship with Him?

_____

_____

_____

How does this apply to my life today?

_____

_____

_____

NOVEMBER 21

The Daily Bible pages 1488–1493

Acts 3:1–6:7

Key events, teaching, or concept:

_____

_____

_____

_____

_____

Key verses:

_____

_____

_____

What is God telling me about Himself or my relationship with Him?

_____

_____

_____

_____

How does this apply to my life today?

_____

_____

_____

_____

The Daily Bible pages 1493–1496

Acts 6:8–8:1

Key events, teaching, or concept:

Key verses:

What is God telling me about Himself or my relationship with Him?

How does this apply to my life today?

The Daily Bible **pages 1496–1500**

Acts 8:1–9:31

Key events, teaching, or concept:

Key verses:

What is God telling me about Himself or my relationship with Him?

How does this apply to my life today?

NOVEMBER 24

The Daily Bible pages 1500–1506

Acts 9:32–12:25

Key events, teaching, or concept:

_____
_____
_____
_____
_____

Key verses:

_____
_____
_____

What is God telling me about Himself or my relationship with Him?

_____
_____
_____
_____

How does this apply to my life today?

_____
_____
_____
_____

NOVEMBER 25

The Daily Bible pages 1506–1512

Acts 13:1–15:35

Key events, teaching, or concept:

Key verses:

What is God telling me about Himself or my relationship with Him?

How does this apply to my life today?

NOVEMBER 26

The Daily Bible pages 1513–1519

Galatians

Key events, teaching, or concept:

_____

_____

_____

_____

_____

Key verses:

_____

_____

_____

What is God telling me about Himself or my relationship with Him?

_____

_____

_____

How does this apply to my life today?

_____

_____

_____

NOVEMBER 27

The Daily Bible pages 1519–1523

Acts 15:36–18:11

Key events, teaching, or concept:

Key verses:

What is God telling me about Himself or my relationship with Him?

How does this apply to my life today?

NOVEMBER 28

The Daily Bible pages 1524–1527

1 Thessalonians

Key events, teaching, or concept:

Key verses:

What is God telling me about Himself or my relationship with Him?

How does this apply to my life today?

The Daily Bible pages 1527–1531

2 Thessalonians

Key events, teaching, or concept:

Key verses:

What is God telling me about Himself or my relationship with Him?

How does this apply to my life today?

NOVEMBER 30

The Daily Bible pages 1531–1535

1 Corinthians 1–4

Key events, teaching, or concept:

Key verses:

What is God telling me about Himself or my relationship with Him?

How does this apply to my life today?

DECEMBER 1

The Daily Bible pages 1535–1542

1 Corinthians 5:1–11:16

Key events, teaching, or concept:

Key verses:

What is God telling me about Himself or my relationship with Him?

How does this apply to my life today?

DECEMBER 2

The Daily Bible pages 1542–1546

1 Corinthians 11:17–14:40

Key events, teaching, or concept:

_____

_____

_____

_____

_____

Key verses:

_____

_____

_____

What is God telling me about Himself or my relationship with Him?

_____

_____

_____

_____

How does this apply to my life today?

_____

_____

_____

_____

DECEMBER 3

The Daily Bible pages 1546–1550

1 Corinthians 15–16; Acts 19:23-41; 20:1

Key events, teaching, or concept:

_____

_____

_____

_____

_____

Key verses:

_____

_____

_____

What is God telling me about Himself or my relationship with Him?

_____

_____

_____

_____

How does this apply to my life today?

_____

_____

_____

_____

DECEMBER 4

The Daily Bible pages 1550–1557

2 Corinthians 1–9

Key events, teaching, or concept:

_____

_____

_____

_____

_____

Key verses:

_____

_____

_____

What is God telling me about Himself or my relationship with Him?

_____

_____

_____

_____

How does this apply to my life today?

_____

_____

_____

_____

DECEMBER 5

The Daily Bible pages 1557–1561

2 Corinthians 10–13; Acts 20:2-3

Key events, teaching, or concept:

Key verses:

What is God telling me about Himself or my relationship with Him?

How does this apply to my life today?

DECEMBER 6

The Daily Bible pages 1561–1565

Romans 1:1–3:20

Key events, teaching, or concept:

_____

_____

_____

_____

_____

Key verses:

_____

_____

_____

What is God telling me about Himself or my relationship with Him?

_____

_____

_____

_____

How does this apply to my life today?

_____

_____

_____

_____

DECEMBER 7

The Daily Bible pages 1565–1571

Romans 3:21–8:39

Key events, teaching, or concept:

_____

_____

_____

_____

_____

Key verses:

_____

_____

_____

What is God telling me about Himself or my relationship with Him?

_____

_____

_____

_____

How does this apply to my life today?

_____

_____

_____

DECEMBER 8

The Daily Bible pages 1571–1575

Romans 9–11

Key events, teaching, or concept:

Key verses:

What is God telling me about Himself or my relationship with Him?

How does this apply to my life today?

DECEMBER 9

The Daily Bible pages 1576–1581

Romans 12

Key events, teaching, or concept:

_____

_____

_____

_____

_____

Key verses:

_____

_____

_____

What is God telling me about Himself or my relationship with Him?

_____

_____

_____

_____

How does this apply to my life today?

_____

_____

_____

_____

DECEMBER 10

The Daily Bible **pages 1581–1583**

Acts 20:3-38; 21:1-16

Key events, teaching, or concept:

_____

_____

_____

_____

_____

Key verses:

_____

_____

_____

What is God telling me about Himself or my relationship with Him?

_____

_____

_____

_____

How does this apply to my life today?

_____

_____

_____

_____

DECEMBER 11

The Daily Bible pages 1583–1587

Acts 21:17–23:35

Key events, teaching, or concept:

_____

_____

_____

_____

_____

_____

Key verses:

_____

_____

_____

_____

What is God telling me about Himself or my relationship with Him?

_____

_____

_____

_____

How does this apply to my life today?

_____

_____

_____

_____

DECEMBER 12

The Daily Bible **pages 1587–1592**

Acts 24–26

Key events, teaching, or concept:

_____

_____

_____

_____

_____

Key verses:

_____

_____

_____

What is God telling me about Himself or my relationship with Him?

_____

_____

_____

_____

How does this apply to my life today?

_____

_____

_____

_____

DECEMBER 13

The Daily Bible pages 1592–1596

Acts 27–28

Key events, teaching, or concept:

_____

_____

_____

_____

_____

Key verses:

_____

_____

_____

What is God telling me about Himself or my relationship with Him?

_____

_____

_____

_____

How does this apply to my life today?

_____

_____

_____

DECEMBER 14

The Daily Bible pages 1596–1601

Colossians; Philemon

Key events, teaching, or concept:

_____

_____

_____

_____

_____

Key verses:

_____

_____

_____

What is God telling me about Himself or my relationship with Him?

_____

_____

_____

How does this apply to my life today?

_____

_____

_____

DECEMBER 15

The Daily Bible pages 1601–1607

Ephesians

Key events, teaching, or concept:

_____

_____

_____

_____

_____

Key verses:

_____

_____

_____

What is God telling me about Himself or my relationship with Him?

_____

_____

_____

_____

How does this apply to my life today?

_____

_____

_____

DECEMBER 16

The Daily Bible **pages 1608–1612**

Philippians

Key events, teaching, or concept:

_____

_____

_____

_____

_____

Key verses:

_____

_____

_____

What is God telling me about Himself or my relationship with Him?

_____

_____

_____

_____

How does this apply to my life today?

_____

_____

_____

_____

DECEMBER 17

The Daily Bible pages 1613–1618

1 Timothy

Key events, teaching, or concept:

_____

_____

_____

_____

_____

Key verses:

_____

_____

_____

What is God telling me about Himself or my relationship with Him?

_____

_____

_____

_____

How does this apply to my life today?

_____

_____

_____

DECEMBER 18

The Daily Bible pages 1618–1620

Titus

Key events, teaching, or concept:

_____

_____

_____

_____

_____

Key verses:

_____

_____

_____

What is God telling me about Himself or my relationship with Him?

_____

_____

_____

How does this apply to my life today?

_____

_____

_____

The Daily Bible pages 1620–1624

2 Timothy

Key events, teaching, or concept:

Key verses:

What is God telling me about Himself or my relationship with Him?

How does this apply to my life today?

The Daily Bible **pages 1624–1630**

James; Jude

Key events, teaching, or concept:

_____

_____

_____

_____

_____

Key verses:

_____

_____

_____

What is God telling me about Himself or my relationship with Him?

_____

_____

_____

_____

How does this apply to my life today?

_____

_____

_____

_____

DECEMBER 21

The Daily Bible pages 1631–1636

1 Peter

Key events, teaching, or concept:

_____

_____

_____

_____

_____

Key verses:

_____

_____

_____

What is God telling me about Himself or my relationship with Him?

_____

_____

_____

_____

How does this apply to my life today?

_____

_____

_____

DECEMBER 22

The Daily Bible pages 1636–1640

2 Peter

Key events, teaching, or concept:

_____

_____

_____

_____

_____

Key verses:

_____

_____

_____

What is God telling me about Himself or my relationship with Him?

_____

_____

_____

How does this apply to my life today?

_____

_____

_____

The Daily Bible pages 1640–1646

Hebrews 1:1–6:12

Key events, teaching, or concept:

_____

_____

_____

_____

_____

Key verses:

_____

_____

_____

What is God telling me about Himself or my relationship with Him?

_____

_____

_____

_____

How does this apply to my life today?

_____

_____

_____

Key events, teaching, or concept:

Key verses:

What is God telling me about Himself or my relationship with Him?

How does this apply to my life today?

DECEMBER 25

The Daily Bible pages 1650–1656

Hebrews 10:19–13:25

Key events, teaching, or concept:

Key verses:

What is God telling me about Himself or my relationship with Him?

How does this apply to my life today?

DECEMBER 26

The Daily Bible **pages 1656–1663**

1 John, 2 John, 3 John

Key events, teaching, or concept:

_____

_____

_____

_____

_____

Key verses:

_____

_____

_____

What is God telling me about Himself or my relationship with Him?

_____

_____

_____

How does this apply to my life today?

_____

_____

_____

DECEMBER 27

The Daily Bible pages 1663–1667

Revelation 1–3

Key events, teaching, or concept:

_____

_____

_____

_____

_____

Key verses:

_____

_____

_____

What is God telling me about Himself or my relationship with Him?

_____

_____

_____

_____

How does this apply to my life today?

_____

_____

_____

DECEMBER 28

The Daily Bible pages 1667–1672

Revelation 4:1–8:6

Key events, teaching, or concept:

_____

_____

_____

_____

_____

Key verses:

_____

_____

_____

What is God telling me about Himself or my relationship with Him?

_____

_____

_____

_____

How does this apply to my life today?

_____

_____

_____

DECEMBER 29

The Daily Bible pages 1672–1677

Revelation 8:7–13:18

Key events, teaching, or concept:

Key verses:

What is God telling me about Himself or my relationship with Him?

How does this apply to my life today?

DECEMBER 30

The Daily Bible pages 1677–1683

Revelation 14:1–19:5

Key events, teaching, or concept:

_____

_____

_____

_____

_____

Key verses:

_____

_____

_____

What is God telling me about Himself or my relationship with Him?

_____

_____

_____

_____

How does this apply to my life today?

_____

_____

_____

DECEMBER 31

The Daily Bible **pages 1683–1688**

Revelation 19:6–22:21

Key events, teaching, or concept:

Key verses:

What is God telling me about Himself or my relationship with Him?

How does this apply to my life today?

THE DAILY BIBLE® SERIES

Compiled and narrated by F. LaGard Smith

The Daily Bible® is available with paperback, hardcover, and imitation leather bindings.

30 Days Through the Bible

Easy-to-read key passages, biblical insights, and devotions explore God's plan, His message, and Scripture's relevance for daily living.

30 Days Through Psalms and Proverbs

In a chapter for each day of the month, LaGard Smith provides succinct and dynamic insight into vital aspects of everyday life, followed by generous portions from the Psalms and Proverbs.

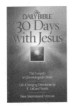

30 Days with Jesus

In this life-changing Bible study, Smith integrates the four gospels into one chronological narrative to highlight the character and attributes of Jesus. Introduction sections give readers an in-depth look into the on-earth ministry of Christ.

Henrietta Smith
God is Able.